HOPE BEYOND THE ELECT

Revisiting Early Christian Views on Prophecy and Salvation

JONATHAN RAMACHANDRAN

HOPE BEYOND THE ELECT

Revisiting Early Christian Views on Prophecy and Salvation

Jonathan Ramachandran

Christian Publishing House

Cambridge, Ohio

HOPE BEYOND THE ELECT: Revisiting Early Christian Views on Prophecy and Salvation by Jonathan Ramachandran

ISBN-13: **978-1-949586-40-4**

Table of Contents

Preface

In every generation, believers have wrestled with questions about the final destiny of mankind, the nature of judgment, and the hope found in Christ. *Hope Beyond the Elect* is not written for theologians alone, but for every sincere Christian who wants to understand the Bible more deeply in light of the earliest preserved teachings of the Church. This work reflects years of study and reflection on the writings of early Christian leaders—many of whom believed and taught Chiliasm, or the literal Millennial Reign of Christ.

Though the original version of this book was written as a scholarly volume, this new edition has been simplified without compromising the biblical doctrine, interpretive method, or convictions held throughout. It is now structured and presented for the average churchgoer who desires clarity without losing theological depth. While some chapters explore deep prophetic themes, all are anchored in the plain teachings of Scripture and supported with direct quotations from the earliest Christian writers whose voices remain preserved in history.

One of the key themes throughout this work is the possibility of what I call **Non-Elect Salvation**—the idea that some may be saved outside the Elect Bride of Christ, but only through a path of divine judgment and cleansing. Though this view is not commonly taught today, several early Christian voices—men like Justin Martyr, Irenaeus, Clement of Alexandria, and others—hinted at a more layered view of salvation than modern systems often acknowledge. By comparing their words with Scripture, I present this idea as a **possibility**, not a dogma, encouraging readers to test all things carefully.

I've chosen to rely only on literal Bible translation philosophy and the **historical-grammatical method** of interpretation. No allegorizing or speculative typology is used. Everything here is based either on the **plain meaning of the Bible** or **quotes from the early Church Fathers** themselves, avoiding modern denominational overlays and theological systems foreign to the ancient texts.

This edition is not exhaustive but faithful. I do not claim perfection. Some interpretations presented here may be right, others may not be. Yet, everything is offered in sincerity, with reverence for the truth of God's Word and the witness of early Christian history. My aim is not to speculate, but to lay out the evidence and draw reasoned conclusions from it—always aware that the Lord alone will reveal all truth in the Day of His judgment.

To those reading this with a heart to seek Jehovah and follow Christ more faithfully, may these pages serve as a tool for deeper understanding, firmer conviction, and enduring hope. Whether one accepts the possibility of **hope beyond the Elect** or not, the ultimate message remains the same: **Believe in the Lord Jesus Christ and you will be saved** (Acts 16:31). May that truth guide all who read this work.

Jonathan Ramachandran

ACKNOWLEDGEMENTS

I would like to thank God the Father, God the Son (our Lord Jesus Christ), and God the Holy Spirit—our most blessed Trinity—for his unfailing mercy in our errors and for all the good things he has done for us. I thank my family: my father (Ramachandran), my late mother (Grace Selwak Kumari), my uncle (JPS—John Perera Sugumaran), and my brothers (Shankar Timothy and Siralan Joshua) for their support throughout my life. I also express my gratitude to other family members, as well as to both Christian and non-Christian friends (too many to name here), for their visible and invisible support.

Special thanks go to Dr. John W. (Jack) Carter, editor of the distinguished pastoral journal *The American Journal of Biblical Theology* (AJBT), for editing my first journal publication (Essay 1 in this book) and for offering insightful comments on the standards of academic writing.

Last but not least, this work could not have been completed without the skilled hand and brilliance of Mr. Edward D. Andrews, CEO and President of Christian Publishing House, who contributed tremendously to the editing process and the publication of this book.

INTRODUCTION

If the ideas presented in this book prove true on the day of judgment, then all glory belongs to God. But if any of them are found to be incorrect—whether in part or in whole—the responsibility is entirely mine, a result of human weakness. If this work does reflect truth, it may show that God's wisdom sometimes runs counter to the popular theological opinions that many hold. But if it contains error, then it still serves a purpose: to show how even a sincere attempt to interpret Scripture can fall short. Either way, this effort highlights two timeless realities: how difficult it is to interpret the Bible correctly, and how easy it is to go astray.

The Bible is the product of divine genius. It is written in such a way that it allows for deep exploration, which is why so many Christians throughout history—using the same sacred text—have arrived at different conclusions. Their efforts reflect both exegesis (drawing meaning out of the text) and, at times, eisegesis (reading meaning into it). This diversity of interpretation reminds us that the goal is not simply to be opinionated, but to be humble and diligent in the pursuit of biblical truth.

In one correspondence with an academic editor who questioned the assumption of biblical inerrancy often held by pastoral journals, I shared my conviction that the inerrancy of Scripture is foundational. While there are many manuscript variants, only one reading can reflect the original wording, and the others must be attributed to human error or later alteration. For me, textual criticism matters only when the meaning of a verse is at stake. If the core message remains unchanged, then the variant is of little concern.

I once submitted a theological question to a respected academic journal but received no reply. The question was simple: *Has your journal ever published a truly new doctrinal insight—one not previously expressed in any other publication or tradition? If so, could I see that article or at least its abstract?*

In my view, when a journal simply repeats what early church fathers or Protestant reformers already affirmed—especially by revisiting manuscripts without advancing a new understanding—it does not produce fresh theological insight. This book, however, attempts to offer something more. If the conclusions presented here are correct, then they open new paths of interpretation—ideas not found in historical creeds or denominational confessions.

How do we recognize a new theological discovery? It's when no published scholar or historical denomination can be cited as having made the same claim, not even as a possibility. That is what I believe this book represents in part. It draws heavily from Scripture and from the writings of the ancient church fathers, but it arrives at interpretive conclusions that, to the best of my knowledge, no one has yet proposed in the same way.

Many have read the same texts I cite, but few—if any—have interpreted them through the same lens. This makes the interpretation itself the discovery. And that is the ultimate goal of biblical study: not to invent new doctrine, but to uncover what has been overlooked, misread, or forgotten. If that goal is met even in part through this book, then may it bring greater light to those who seek the truth of God's Word with reverence, courage, and clarity.

CHAPTER 1 Hope for the Non-Elect? Exploring Salvation Beyond the Elect

Reflection

It is a gift from God to recognize when something is seriously wrong, even if no one else around us—perhaps not even our own church—sees it. Martin Luther experienced this very thing. Then came the courage to speak out and stand firmly on the Word of God, even at great personal cost. Little could Luther have imagined that his 95 theses, nailed in protest, would eventually ignite the Protestant movement we know today. Now, nearly 40% of Christians worldwide—two out of every five—are the fruit of that bold act of conscience. This is a testimony to God's hand on Luther's life, despite his flaws, and it reminds us that salvation comes from God's mercy through faith in Christ. That same mercy gives us hope, affirming that salvation in Christ is broader and more gracious than we may have dared to imagine.

Introduction

Martin Luther's act of nailing the 95 theses to the church door in Wittenberg was not intended to start a revolution, but to reform the Roman Catholic Church from its extra-biblical traditions. What followed was the birth of the Protestant movement—a continuing effort to recover biblical truth and purity. Despite being unified in many essential beliefs, Protestantism today remains divided on a range of doctrines and practices.

These divisions, while painful at times, may actually serve a purpose. They expose differences that God uses to reveal who is truly approved in his sight (see 1 Corinthians 11:19). The gospel is not simply a message about who Jesus is, but also a call to obey what Jesus taught. In Matthew 7:21–23, Jesus warned that many would claim to have prophesied, cast out demons, and performed miracles in his name, only to hear the devastating reply: "I never knew you." What separates the true disciple from the self-deceived is obedience: "Whoever hears these sayings of Mine and does them…" (Matthew 7:24).

In that spirit, I offer this first of several proposed reforms in our understanding of salvation.

1. Sola Unity in Diversity

Scripture teaches that there are three levels of spiritual fruitfulness in response to the gospel: thirtyfold, sixtyfold, and hundredfold (Matthew 13:8). These represent differing levels of obedience and reward. The implication is significant: believers may hold varying degrees of error and yet still be within the bounds of salvation, based on the measure of faith God has granted to each (Romans 12:3).

1.1 Balancing Tolerance and Doctrinal Conviction

Since the measure of faith is distributed by God, it is neither necessary nor fruitful to force others to adopt every point of our doctrinal understanding. Some may never be able to accept certain truths in this life, even if they are ultimately right. Recognizing this fosters patience and reduces unnecessary conflict within the body of Christ.

Each step toward greater biblical accuracy reflects a deeper relationship with God. At the same time, we must guard against theological pride. There is no place in the church for shaming others over secondary differences. We should be free to express strong convictions, but judgment belongs to God. Our role is to walk in love, honor one another in areas of agreement, and trust God to reward each according to their faithfulness.

Sadly, some Christians distance themselves from others—avoiding collaboration or withholding support—simply because they don't agree on every theological issue. This should not be. Christian freedom allows us to live without causing others to stumble while leaving judgment and reward in God's hands. In this spirit of grace, this essay explores a profound and controversial possibility: that God's mercy may extend even to some who are not part of the elect.

1.2 The Lord Jesus' Parable of the Wheat and the Tares

In one of his most insightful parables, Jesus taught that both the righteous ("wheat") and the unrighteous ("tares") would grow together in the field of the world until the end of the age (Matthew 13:24–30, 36–43). Remarkably, he instructed his followers not to try and remove the tares ahead of time, warning that doing so could cause harm to the wheat as well. This divine command implies that the Church is not tasked with purging all error or hypocrisy from within itself before Christ returns. Instead, the separation belongs to God and will be carried out at the appointed time—at the harvest, when the Son of Man sends forth his angels to gather the righteous into his kingdom.

This approach teaches a posture of **tolerance and humility** within the Church. Jesus clearly expected that false believers would be present among true ones, and that prematurely trying to uproot them might cause damage—possibly even removing faithful servants who appear doubtful or imperfect. Church leaders, therefore, bear great responsibility. If they wrongly judge or exclude someone who is, in fact, genuine wheat, they risk spiritual harm and will be held accountable.

One reason Christ gave this instruction may lie in the nature of human free will. The early Church father **Irenaeus of Lyons** explained that people can change. In his words, "Man, being endowed with reason… having been made free in his will… sometimes becomes wheat, and sometimes chaff." In other words, someone who appears to be a tare today might, by repentance and transformation, become wheat tomorrow.

For that reason, the Church should serve as a cradle of repentance, not a courtroom of condemnation. We must remain open to the possibility that God is still at work in the lives of people we might otherwise dismiss. The patience and restraint Jesus calls for in this parable make space for grace, allowing time for conversion before the final separation at judgment.

This lesson also teaches us to be cautious about overconfidence in our doctrinal positions. If God allowed major errors to persist in the global Church for centuries—such as between 500 AD and 1500 AD—then our own generation, church, or denomination may also hold views that are wrong in part. Our calling is not to elevate our perspective as infallible, but to submit our understanding to the Word of God and test it with humility.

To provide a reliable foundation for evaluating doctrines, we should look to what is **universally affirmed** by the early Christian community. The Nicene Creed of 325 AD, recognized across Catholic, Orthodox, and Protestant traditions, offers a kind of doctrinal boundary. While individual interpretations may vary, this common confession helps preserve the core of the faith from heresy.

Within that boundary, we may examine serious theological questions— such as the possibility of salvation for the non-elect—not with arrogance or reckless speculation, but with reverence, honesty, and a desire to align ourselves more closely with God's truth.

1.3 Non-Elect Salvation Possibility

St. Gregory of Nazianzus once wrote, "Then here too I will provide you with broad paths… about resurrection, about judgment, about reward… For in these subjects to hit the mark is not useless, and to miss it is not dangerous." In this statement, Gregory emphasized that certain theological topics—such as the nature of divine judgment—can be debated without jeopardizing one's salvation. While these ideas may not affect whether someone is saved, they may still affect the **rewards** one receives. This provides space for thoughtful exploration without fear of crossing doctrinal boundaries.

History reminds us that widespread beliefs can be wrong. Martin Luther stood against over a thousand years of Church tradition to restore key biblical truths. So, we must be willing to reexamine doctrines that are widely accepted, especially when strong scriptural evidence invites us to do so.

In that spirit, we return to **1 Corinthians 3:15**, where Paul speaks of a person who is *"saved, yet so as through fire."* While this has often been interpreted as referring to Christian testing in this life—or as purgatory in Catholic theology—there may be another possibility: this person could represent a **non-elect individual** who, while not part of the Church in life, is still saved by God's mercy in the final judgment.

St. Gregory also spoke of a **"last baptism"—a painful, fiery purification**—which could refer to a post-mortem judgment (1 Corinthians 3:12–19). He applied this image to those who did not follow Christ in this life but who might, in the end, be saved through fire. If this reading is correct, it offers a possible framework for understanding **non-elect salvation—** those who are not part of Christ's bride but still receive mercy on Judgment Day.

This interpretation is supported further by the distinction Paul draws between **celestial and terrestrial resurrection bodies** in 1 Corinthians 15:40. Those who receive celestial bodies are the elect, raised in glory to rule with Christ in heaven. But others may be raised to **terrestrial life**—still saved, but in a lesser condition. Their salvation would be real, but it would not carry the glory or reward of those raised with Christ to heavenly rule.

This concept is not universalism. It does not suggest that all will be saved, nor does it affirm the Catholic notion of purgatory. Rather, it opens a third category: people outside the Church who, though they did not follow Christ in life, may respond to him at the judgment—after seeing the truth.

Such a category would explain why Jesus repeatedly described **differing outcomes at the resurrection**, including some who are surprised by their salvation (Matthew 25:31–46) and others who experience **"baptism by fire"**—a painful, refining encounter with divine justice.

While this idea challenges traditional evangelical theology, it is not without precedent. Some early Church Fathers entertained similar possibilities. If salvation truly belongs to God, and if his mercy extends beyond what we can now see or measure, then non-elect salvation becomes not a doctrine, but a **biblically grounded possibility** worth humble consideration.

2.0 Detailed Exploration of a Non-Elect Salvation Possibility

This section delves deeper into the prophetic and theological implications of a controversial question: Could there be salvation for some who are not among the elect? This is not a question to be taken lightly, as it touches on longstanding debates throughout Christian history about judgment, resurrection, and the reach of God's mercy.

Earlier, we considered a quote from **St. Gregory of Nazianzus** that may point to a post-mortem salvation scenario. He described a final, fiery baptism—a painful and prolonged purification—based on **1 Corinthians 3:12–19**, in which even those outside the faith might be cleansed and saved. Gregory addressed not believers in Christ, but *heretics*—those knowingly walking a different path. He did not exclude the possibility that such people, through a last fiery trial, might ultimately receive mercy. This view supports a **non-elect salvation** reading of 1 Corinthians 3:15, where one is "saved, yet so as through fire."

To better understand this interpretation, we must compare **1 Corinthians 3:14 and 3:15**. Verse 14 describes a believer whose work survives and who is rewarded. In contrast, verse 15 depicts a person whose work is entirely burned, who receives **no reward**, yet is still saved—by fire. If we compare this with Jesus' Parable of the Sower in **Matthew 13:8**, those who bear fruit—thirtyfold, sixtyfold, or hundredfold—are Christians who receive rewards. It seems unlikely, then, that a Christian would be saved by fire without reward, as in verse 15, since even minimal faithfulness should result in at least a thirtyfold return.

This opens the possibility that the one saved by fire in 1 Corinthians 3:15 is **not a Christian at all**, but someone outside the elect. If true, the reward-bearing Christian is in view in verse 14, while verse 15 refers to a non-elect person saved with no reward—only by divine mercy.

Some argue that this passage only refers to Christians, based on **1 Corinthians 3:11**, which says that "no one can lay a foundation other than the one already laid, which is Jesus Christ." However, this may also include those who followed the conscience that God placed in them, as discussed in **Romans 2:6–11**, where even Gentiles who do not have the law may still act in accordance with its principles. Paul teaches that *"the doers of the law will be justified"*—suggesting that those who live righteously according to their conscience may be judged mercifully by God, even if they never heard the gospel.

This interpretation aligns with what many early Church Fathers believed. It suggests that Christ's atonement might be extended in the Spirit World to those who were never reached in life. If this is the case, then salvation by fire does not violate the gospel but rather fulfills it in a broader and still Christ-centered way.

Such a view doesn't promote salvation by works. Rather, it affirms that the **application of Christ's atonement** may extend beyond this life for those who never had the chance to hear or understand the gospel. The "fire" may serve as a form of final purging or awakening, making them ready to receive mercy on Judgment Day.

This helps explain why some Church Fathers offered different interpretations of these same verses. The difficulty of this passage invites honest inquiry—and it reminds us that salvation is ultimately in God's hands. This perspective does not replace the gospel message of faith and repentance now, but it opens the door to **hope**—that God's justice and mercy are not bound by human timing.

2.1 Unlearnt and Learnt Cases

The distinction between "unlearnt" and "learnt" individuals is an important framework when considering the possibility of non-elect salvation. These categories refer to those who have never heard the gospel ("unlearnt") and those who have ("learnt").

The apostle Paul, in **Romans 2:12–13**, writes that "all who have sinned without the law will also perish without the law, and all who have sinned under the law will be judged by the law. For it is not the hearers of the law who are righteous before God, but the doers of the law who will be justified." This clearly refers to the **learnt case**—those who have heard God's word. Paul states that justification is possible for those who **do** the works of the law. Some theologians link this passage with the one in **1 Corinthians 3:15**, proposing that these "doers" who fall short may still be saved "as through fire."

However, it's difficult to imagine a faithful Christian—someone who truly believes—receiving **no reward**. Faith itself is a gift of immense worth, and **living faith** necessarily produces fruit. James 2:26 says, "faith without works is dead." Therefore, a true Christian, bearing at least thirtyfold fruit as in Jesus' parable (Matthew 13:8), would align more naturally with the **rewarded** individual of 1 Corinthians 3:14, not the one who is saved by fire with no reward in verse 15.

This raises the possibility that the person in 1 Corinthians 3:15 is not a Christian but a "learnt" individual who heard the gospel yet failed to respond in obedient faith. They might recognize Christ **after death**, not by faith in this life, but upon seeing him in the spirit world. Jesus alluded to this dynamic in **John 6:36, 40**, where he rebuked those who saw him and still refused to believe, but affirmed that *"everyone who sees the Son and believes in him will have eternal life."*

This opens up a theological question: Could some be saved by believing **after seeing** Christ—post-mortem—especially among those who were exposed to the gospel yet failed to respond with faith in this life? Might this correspond to those who are "saved by fire" in a final purifying judgment?

The **unlearnt case** adds further nuance. These are people who lived without ever hearing the gospel. Paul writes in **Romans 2:14–16** that even Gentiles, who do not have the law, can still act in accordance with it by following their conscience. Their moral choices, if aligned with God's principles, may either **accuse or excuse** them on the day of judgment.

This is not a doctrine of salvation by works. Rather, it affirms that the blood of Christ is powerful enough to be applied even to those who never explicitly believed in him during their earthly lives. The Church Fathers sometimes viewed this category with hope, recognizing that Christ's atonement may reach even those who are outside the covenant in this life— but who respond in the spirit world when confronted with the truth.

These two cases—**learnt but unbelieving**, and **unlearnt but morally upright**—could represent distinct classes of those who are ultimately **"saved by fire."** They are not part of the elect, do not receive heavenly rewards, and do not enter into Christ's millennial rule. But they may be raised in the second resurrection to a life of mercy, saved without glory, through the refining judgment of God.

Whether this interpretation proves true or false remains to be seen. It is not asserted as dogma but presented as a sincere exploration of Scripture and early Christian thought. What matters most is that such reflections are offered with honesty and humility—never to distort the gospel, but to seek its depth and extent with reverence.

2.2 Chiliasm Church Fathers

Some of the earliest Christian thinkers—those known today as the **Chiliasm Church Fathers**—offered insights that support the idea of **non-elect salvation**. These leaders, including **Irenaeus of Lyons**, **Justin Martyr**, and **Tertullian**, shared a common view that Christians would participate in a **first resurrection** and reign with Christ for a thousand years in **glorified human bodies**. This millennial reign occurs on the current earth and heavens. At the **end of this reign**, a dramatic transformation takes place, described in Scripture as the change from "flesh and blood" to something **heavenly or angelic**—a change necessary to enter the final, eternal kingdom (cf. 1 Corinthians 15:50–52).

These early church leaders also make important distinctions in how salvation is experienced. According to their writings, **the elect** are raised first, enjoy the blessings of the thousand-year reign with Christ, and are eventually transformed into a **celestial existence** to dwell in the New Heaven. But others, described as the **"nations who are saved"** in Revelation 21:24, are mentioned as being distinct from the Bride (the Church). These individuals are not raised to rule with Christ, nor are they immediately granted celestial glory, but they are saved and enter the new earth in **terrestrial (earthly) resurrection bodies**.

This distinction supports the idea that not all who are saved are part of the elect. Some may receive a **lower-grade salvation**—granted by God's mercy but without the privilege of reigning with Christ or sharing in His heavenly nature. This aligns with the **Chiliasm** view, where prophecy is not to be interpreted privately (2 Peter 1:20), and the writings of these earliest fathers are considered vital testimony to God's intentions for the end times.

It's worth noting that **Chiliasm prophecy** places the transformation into heavenly glory **not** at the beginning of the millennium, but at its **conclusion**, when the Bride becomes one flesh with Christ. The Book of

Revelation shows the **Bride descending from heaven**, while the nations walk by her light. This indicates that the Bride and the nations are **not the same group**. The Bride possesses **celestial bodies**; the saved nations do not.

These early writers believed the Church was raised to life in glorified human bodies to live and reign with Christ for 1,000 years in justice and peace. Then, at the **last trumpet**, this same Church is changed into **no longer flesh and blood**, so it may enter heaven. This helps make sense of the "Water of Life" imagery in Revelation 22. The saved nations drink from this water; the Bride no longer needs to, for she partakes of life from Christ directly.

This framework fits with the larger theme of **God's layered mercy**— first shown to the elect who believe and follow Christ in this life, and later shown to others who respond in repentance, even if after death. The non-elect may be purified through judgment and raised into an earthly kingdom, a mercy that does not contradict justice but magnifies grace.

In conclusion, the teachings of the **Chiliasm Church Fathers** provide historical and theological support for the possibility of **non-elect salvation**. While not widely accepted in modern Christianity, these ancient voices compel us to consider that God's mercy may reach further than many expect, especially in the final age to come.

2.3 Chiliasm Prophecy Regarding Change from Human to Angelic

In the final chapters of the Bible, a powerful image emerges: the **Bride of Christ**—the elect Church—is seen calling others to salvation, inviting them to take the **Water of Life freely** (Revelation 22:17). This invitation, coming from the Bride, implies that there are still others outside of her number who are being saved. These are not the elect but may represent the "nations who are saved" (Revelation 21:24), who live on the new earth while the Bride resides in the New Jerusalem.

According to **Chiliasm prophecy**, Christians are raised in **resurrected human bodies** to reign with Christ for 1,000 years on the old earth and heavens—the same world in which they suffered for their faith. This reward fits the justice of God, repaying the faithful with life and honor in the very realm where they were mistreated.

However, at the **end** of that thousand-year reign, a transformation occurs. The Bride—the faithful Church—is changed into a new kind of being: no longer flesh and blood, but **angelic and heavenly**. This transformation allows them to inherit the New Heaven, where "flesh and blood cannot inherit the kingdom of God" (1 Corinthians 15:50). During the millennial reign, the elect drink from the Water of Life to sustain their human but glorified bodies. But after this transformation, they no longer need it, for they become **"one flesh" with Christ**, drawing life directly from him.

In contrast, those who are not part of the Bride—the "nations of those who are saved"—continue to **drink from the Water of Life** in their **terrestrial (earthly)** resurrection bodies. They live in the new earth, not the New Jerusalem, and do not experience the same transformation as the elect. Yet, they are still saved. This interpretation opens the door to understanding these saved nations as possible recipients of **non-elect salvation**—not glorified in the same way as the Church, but welcomed into eternal life by God's mercy.

This distinction between **celestial and terrestrial resurrection bodies** was affirmed by some of the earliest Church Fathers. Their understanding of the timeline aligns with this view: the transformation from human to angelic does not happen at the start of the millennium, but **at its end**, at the sounding of the "last trumpet." During the 1,000 years, the elect rule in resurrected, sinless human bodies. Then, when Christ fully unites with his Bride, they are changed to heavenly, immortal beings.

This reading stands in contrast to many modern interpretations—whether Protestant, Catholic, or Orthodox—which often conflate the resurrection with the final transformation. The **Chiliasm Fathers** believed otherwise: that the resurrection to human life comes first, followed later by the transformation into angelic life. This interpretation not only supports the distinction between elect and non-elect salvation, but also fits closely with the flow of biblical prophecy.

Interestingly, even **St. Augustine**, often critical of Chiliasm, seems to have retained a similar understanding: that the righteous will undergo a transformation from human to angelic after the millennium. If so, this insight may not be exclusive to Chiliasm but a remnant of early apostolic teaching preserved in part through Augustine's theology.

While this interpretation cannot be proven until prophecy is fulfilled, the testimony of early Christian voices—those closest to the apostles—should not be lightly dismissed. Their unified vision of a **two-stage glorification** offers compelling support for the idea that **God's mercy may include some who are not elect**, saving them in the resurrection with an earthly body while reserving celestial glory for the Bride alone.

2.4 Chiliasm Prophecy for the Timeline of the Last Trumpet

According to the **Chiliasm Church Fathers**, the prophecy concerning the "last trumpet" holds significant implications for how and when the resurrection of the dead unfolds—and particularly how it may relate to the possibility of **non-elect salvation**. Among these early voices, **Victorinus of Pettau** and **Irenaeus of Lyons** give special attention to **1 Corinthians 15:52**, the only verse in Scripture that specifically mentions the "last trumpet."

Victorinus places this trumpet at the **end of the 1,000-year reign** of Christ. In his view, those who were not part of the first resurrection—namely, the elect who reign with Christ—are raised at this last trumpet. He writes that these others, who were not previously raised, will rise at the end of the millennium "among the impious and sinners." Yet even within this group, there appears to be a **second badge of the righteous**, individuals distinct from the wicked, who are raised at the same time. This raises the question: who are these righteous that appear only at the second resurrection?

Irenaeus may offer insight here. He refers to the possibility of some of Christ's **enemies or opponents** being saved. This aligns with Jesus' own teaching in **Matthew 25**, where the "sheep" are surprised to find themselves welcomed into the kingdom. They had unknowingly served Christ by caring for his brethren. These sheep of the nations may not have known the Lord in this life—but the Lord knew them, recognizing their acts of love and mercy.

Under the **Chiliasm timeline**, the elect are already saved and reigning during the 1,000 years. At the end of that reign—on the Day of Judgment—those of the second resurrection are raised, both the wicked and these surprised sheep. This supports the idea that some may be saved **after death**, not as members of the Bride, but as recipients of God's mercy based on how they treated his people.

Jesus' words in **John 5** seem to suggest this dual timeline. He speaks of two moments: *"The hour is coming, and now is"*—which likely refers to the **first resurrection**—and later, *"the hour is coming"*—which may point to the **second resurrection**. These distinctions imply a staged resurrection process, with the second group being judged and possibly saved at the **last trumpet**, in harmony with both 1 Corinthians 15 and Revelation 20.

This view is further supported by the early Church's belief that prophecy is not subject to private interpretation (2 Peter 1:20). The consistent voice of multiple early fathers—including **Victorinus**, **Tertullian**, and **Irenaeus**—adds weight to the interpretation that the final trumpet signals a **second resurrection** with mixed results: judgment for some, salvation for others.

If correct, this interpretation lends credibility to the **non-elect salvation possibility**—that at the last trumpet, some may be saved who were not believers during their earthly lives. They do not receive the celestial, angelic bodies prepared for the elect, but they are raised in earthly, terrestrial bodies and live in the **new earth**, not in the **New Jerusalem**. Their salvation is real, though **without glory**, in contrast to the glorified Church.

This layered view of the resurrection helps explain how God may offer both **justice** and **mercy**—rewarding the faithful who followed Christ in life and showing compassion to others who, though outside the Church, demonstrated love toward his people. It encourages us to maintain a high view of salvation while remaining humble about the limits of our understanding.

2.5 Evidence in the Book of 1 Enoch

The Book of 1 Enoch—though not part of the Protestant canon—is considered canonical by the Ethiopian Orthodox Church and valued by early Jewish and Christian traditions. In **Chapter 50**, it presents a vivid prophetic scene that may lend support to the **Chiliasm framework** and, by extension, the possibility of **non-elect salvation**.

The chapter opens with a dramatic transformation of the *"elect"* (understood here as faithful Christians). These are described as receiving a **change**—from earthly, human existence to a glorious, shining form with the *"light of days,"* implying the glorification of their resurrection bodies. This echoes Paul's teaching in **1 Corinthians 15:52**, where the dead are raised incorruptible at the "last trumpet" and changed.

But more striking is what happens in **verse 3**, which seems to describe a **second group**: individuals who are saved *through* the name of the Lord, but who are said to have *"no honour."* This is a remarkable distinction. Unlike the elect who are glorified, these are saved without glory—suggesting a different kind of salvation, one not characterized by ruling with Christ or receiving heavenly reward. It cannot refer to the elect, as the elect are consistently described in Scripture as being honored and rewarded (cf. Revelation 20:4–6).

The text reads:

"They shall have no honour through the name of the Lord of Spirits, yet through His name shall they be saved, and the Lord of Spirits will have compassion on them, for His compassion is great."

This opens the door to what might be called **non-elect salvation**: individuals who are not glorified, yet receive divine mercy. Their salvation is real but lacks the reward and position granted to the elect. The text implies that this mercy comes *after judgment*, for the next verses describe the fate of those who do not repent:

"At His judgment the unrepentant shall perish before Him. And from henceforth I will have no mercy on them," says the Lord of Spirits.

This sets a clear boundary. Mercy is available—even to some sinners— up to a certain point. But after that, judgment is final. The mercy shown to the repentant *non-elect* occurs **before** this final cutoff. These individuals respond in repentance after **witnessing the glory of the elect**, a concept that resembles the idea of *believing after seeing*—a post-mortem repentance scenario not traditionally included in Protestant theology, yet one that does not inherently conflict with the justice of God.

This interpretation aligns with the **Second Resurrection** timeline in Revelation 20. Those who are part of the **first resurrection** reign with Christ; those who arise later face judgment. The Book of 1 Enoch may be referring to this latter group—sinners who, upon seeing the truth, respond in repentance and are granted salvation without the honor of heavenly reward.

If preserved accurately, this portion of 1 Enoch adds weight to the argument that **non-elect salvation is both ancient and theologically conceivable**. It offers a hopeful glimpse into God's mercy, showing that while not all are glorified, some may still be saved.

2.6 Earliest Chiliasm Quotes

To explore the foundation of non-elect salvation within early Christian thought, we must consider the voices of the earliest **Chiliasm Church Fathers**—especially **St. Papias, St. Justin Martyr,** and **St. Irenaeus of Lyons**. These early witnesses present a vision of prophecy and eschatology that supports a **graded view of salvation**, with distinctions between those who are rewarded with heavenly glory and others who are saved without such honor.

St. Papias, bishop of Hierapolis (c. 60–163 AD), is one of the most significant sources in this regard. Described by **Irenaeus** as a hearer of the apostle John and a companion of Polycarp, Papias's proximity to the apostles gives his testimony weight. According to his writings, all Christians—those who produce thirtyfold, sixtyfold, or hundredfold fruit—will take part in the **wedding of the Lamb** and inherit a place in **heaven**. However, Papias also describes heaven itself as being **layered**, with different levels of proximity to divine glory.

He writes that some dwell in the **New Jerusalem**, others in the **Paradise level**, and others in **outer heavenly regions**. These distinctions seem to correlate to the fruitfulness scale given by Jesus in **Matthew 13:8**, where different believers bear different amounts of fruit and are thus rewarded differently. Importantly, this layered view does not deny anyone salvation but affirms that **salvation and reward are not the same**.

The concept of **layered heavens** also aligns with **2 Corinthians 12:2**, where Paul speaks of being caught up to the "third heaven." Though the Bible does not elaborate further, early Christian and Jewish writings expand this idea, suggesting that the first and second heavens refer to realms of lesser glory. This harmonizes with Papias's description of different heavenly zones—allowing room for saved individuals who do not receive the **fullness of elect reward**.

These ideas reinforce the concept that there may be those saved **outside the Bride**, saved not as heirs but as inhabitants—granted eternal life, yet without the intimacy and glory reserved for the elect. Their salvation, while genuine, lacks the **celestial inheritance** described for the Church in texts like **Revelation 21–22**.

This interpretation strengthens the framework for **non-elect salvation**. It is not universalism; it is a measured mercy. These individuals are not judged with the wicked but are also not raised in the first resurrection. They do not partake in Christ's millennial reign, nor are they called "priests" or "kings," as Revelation 20:6 describes of the elect.

In this light, the earliest Chiliasm Fathers present a consistent theme: **salvation by degrees**, administered according to divine justice and mercy. Not all will enter heaven in the same way, and not all will receive the same glory. Some, though saved, will remain in **terrestrial resurrection bodies** on the new earth, while others—the elect—will dwell in **celestial bodies**, transformed and glorified to share in Christ's divine nature.

This concept is echoed in **Justin Martyr's** writings, who envisioned a bodily resurrection with subsequent reward based on faith and works. **Irenaeus** carried this further, using analogies from Israel's inheritance and emphasizing the distinction between those who are saved to eternal life and those who are **let go free**—a phrase that may refer to **non-elect mercy.**

Ultimately, this early testimony affirms what Scripture implies: that **God is just**, rewarding every person according to their works (Romans 2:6–10), and that **salvation is multi-dimensional**, with distinctions based on faithfulness, revelation, and divine purpose. These ancient quotes do not contradict the gospel—they deepen our understanding of how salvation may extend beyond our current theological categories.

2.8 St. Augustine of Hippo and His View on Eschatological Heresy

St. Augustine of Hippo (354–430 AD) remains one of the most influential figures in Christian theology, revered by Catholics, Orthodox, and Protestants alike. What many do not realize, however, is that his teacher and baptizer was **St. Ambrose of Milan**—a Church Father who expressed hope for the salvation of all people, including those outside the visible Church.

Ambrose once wrote: *"Now, since all do not believe, all do not seem to be in subjection. But when all have believed and done the will of God, then Christ will be all in all. And when Christ is all in all, then God will be all in all."* This quote influenced the post–Vatican II **Catholic Catechism**, which affirms the Church's hope for the salvation of all humanity: *"In hope, the Church prays for all men to be saved."*

What makes Augustine particularly interesting is that he did not brand **Christian universalists**—those who believed in a temporary hell and eventual restoration—as heretics. This is notable, given that Church Fathers in his era were generally quick to label false teachers. In fact, Augustine allowed for the possibility of **relief or intermission of torment** for the damned. He recognized that some people might be saved *outside* the kingdom of God—perhaps alluding to a form of **non-elect salvation**, in which some souls are ultimately spared eternal condemnation, even if they are not glorified with Christ.

In his writing, Augustine admits:

"It is in vain, then, that some, indeed very many, make moan over the eternal punishment... Let them suppose, if the thought gives them pleasure, that the pains of the damned are, at certain intervals, in some degree assuaged... Though His tender mercies are exhibited, not in putting an end to their eternal punishment, but in mitigating, or in granting them a respite from, their torments."

Although Augustine does not endorse universalism, he does not rule out **God's mercy reaching into judgment** in ways that remain mysterious. He entertains the possibility that some might be saved after a form of *purgatorial fire*, even suggesting that the degree of punishment correlates with how deeply one loved the goods of the world. Those who were overly attached might suffer longer; those who practiced more charity might be delivered sooner.

In another work, Augustine writes:

"It is a matter that may be inquired into… whether some believers shall pass through a kind of purgatorial fire… and in proportion as they have loved with more or less devotion the goods that perish, be less or more quickly delivered from it."

He further notes that such purification is only possible for those who do not fall into the category of the damned—those who *will not inherit the kingdom of God* unless their sins are forgiven through repentance.

Augustine thus provides a helpful model for approaching the **non-elect salvation possibility.** He does not affirm it as doctrine, but he does not reject it as heresy. Rather, he allows space for **gradations in punishment** and **shades of mercy**, leaving room for God to show compassion even toward those outside the boundaries of the elect.

From a Protestant standpoint, it would be difficult to argue that Augustine—or his teacher Ambrose—was unsaved. Yet both men entertained thoughts that resemble the concept of **non-elect salvation:** mercy shown to sinners beyond the first resurrection, beyond the rewards of the faithful, but still within God's redemptive purpose.

This gives Christians today the freedom to **discuss these possibilities** without fear of condemnation. The goal is not to dilute the gospel or deny the urgency of repentance, but to consider whether God's mercy might extend in ways that are biblically and historically plausible—especially in light of figures like Augustine who remained within the boundaries of orthodoxy while pondering such matters.

2.9 Possible Scripture-Level Vision – Shepherd of Hermas

The *Shepherd of Hermas*—also known as *The Pastor*—was regarded with significant reverence by many early Christians. Some Church Fathers, including **St. Irenaeus of Lyons** and **Tertullian**, even treated it as Scripture or near-Scripture. It appeared in early canonical collections like the **Muratorian Canon** (c. 170 AD) in the West and the **Codex Sinaiticus** (4th century) in the East. Though later excluded from formal canon lists, its early reception shows that it held authoritative weight for generations of Christians.

The *Shepherd* speaks allegorically of salvation through imagery like the **Tower of Repentance**, representing the Church. Those who are chosen and faithful are depicted as **fitting stones** placed securely in this tower—the elect. This metaphor was also cited by Irenaeus, who called the Church a "beautiful elect tower" raised across the world and filled with those who receive the Spirit.

However, the same vision reveals a remarkable extension of mercy beyond the elect. The narrative introduces **rejected stones**—people who had once heard the gospel and desired baptism, but fell back into sinful lifestyles. These individuals are not placed into the tower. Instead, the angel explains:

"Repentance is yet possible, but in this tower, they cannot find a suitable place. But in another and much inferior place they will be laid, and that too only when they have been tortured and completed the days of their sins. And on this account will they be transferred, because they have partaken of the righteous Word."

These words indicate the possibility of a **non-elect salvation**: a place of redemption not within the Church proper (the tower), but in a lesser realm of mercy. The condition? Repentance must arise *during or after* their suffering, and only because they once engaged with the Word of God. This is not universal salvation. Not all are saved. The passage clearly states that if the desire to repent does not arise, they **will not** be saved—because of the hardness of their hearts.

This vision bears resemblance to **1 Corinthians 3:15**, where someone is "saved, yet so as through fire." Here, too, salvation is preceded by judgment, and the saved are not rewarded. Some have linked this with Jesus' teaching about being baptized "with fire" (Matthew 3:11–12), suggesting this could involve purification through suffering, not just for the elect but also potentially for others.

Tertullian, although critical of the *Shepherd*'s doctrine regarding adulterers, still acknowledged its spiritual authority. In debate with Pope Callixtus I, he wrote:

"I would yield my ground to you, if the Scripture of the Shepherd, which is the only one that favors adulterers, had deserved to find a place in the

Divine canon… I, however, imbibe the Scriptures of that Shepherd who cannot be broken."

While expressing discomfort with certain aspects of the text, Tertullian still accepted the *Shepherd of Hermas* as a meaningful spiritual work. His cautious engagement highlights the sincerity with which the early Church wrestled with such ideas.

It is worth noting that **St. Athanasius**, who formalized the New Testament canon in his 39th Festal Letter, did not include the *Shepherd* as canonical. Yet he placed it on the same level as **Esther**—implying significant value. The Roman Canon had likewise affirmed it should be read, though not publicly in church. No known council ever condemned the text; it simply faded from usage over time.

From a theological standpoint, the distinction between salvation **inside** the tower (elect) and salvation **outside** the tower (non-elect) could correspond to the biblical categories of those who enter the **New Heaven** (Revelation 21:2) and those who dwell on the **New Earth** (Revelation 21:24). The *Shepherd* may describe the latter—those saved, but not glorified.

Ultimately, the *Shepherd of Hermas* offers a unique early Christian vision of **hope beyond exclusion**. Its parables suggest that God's mercy may reach even those who fail to persevere in faith, so long as they repent—even if only after judgment begins. Though the Church rightly upholds salvation through Christ as the only way, it may be that his reach extends even further than we have imagined.

2.10 Rabbinical Judaism and Its Two Types of Proselytes

Rabbinical Judaism distinguishes between two categories of converts, or **proselytes**: the *ger tzedek* ("righteous proselyte") and the *ger toshav* ("resident alien" or "limited proselyte"). The *ger tzedek* is considered a full convert, obligated to keep the entire Torah, while the *ger toshav* is only expected to follow the **Seven Laws of Noah**. These seven commandments, drawn from **Babylonian Talmud Sanhedrin 56a–b** and **Tosefta Avodah Zarah 9:4**, include prohibitions against idolatry, blasphemy, murder, sexual immorality, theft, eating flesh torn from a living animal, and failing to establish courts of justice.

According to rabbinic tradition, those who observe these seven laws are assured "a portion in the world to come." This opens an interesting parallel with the idea of **non-elect salvation**. These *Noahide Gentiles* are not covenant members in the sense of Israel or the Church, but they are considered

righteous among the nations. Their obedience, though partial, is deemed sufficient for God's favor. This aligns with the possibility that some may be saved **outside the covenant** but **within God's mercy**, a central theme of this essay.

Jesus' **Parable of the Good Samaritan** (Luke 10:25–37) may offer a Christ-centered reflection of this concept. The Samaritan was not part of the religious establishment and, according to Jesus (John 4:22), Samaritans *"worship what they do not know."* Yet the Samaritan's mercy and kindness stood in stark contrast to the priest and Levite. By presenting the Samaritan as the model of neighborly love, Jesus affirms that **acts of mercy—even from outsiders—can reflect divine righteousness**.

This raises the possibility that the *ger toshav*, or limited proselyte, may be comparable to the **"surprised sheep"** in Matthew 25:31–46. These are individuals who serve the least of Christ's brothers without knowing they are serving Christ. When the Lord praises them and welcomes them into the kingdom, they respond, *'Lord, when did we see you…?'*—indicating that their salvation was not based on conscious faith, but on **deeds of compassion** toward Christians, whom Christ identifies as his own.

If this interpretation holds, it suggests that the righteous Gentiles—those who fulfill the Noahide laws or the moral core of the last six of the Ten Commandments—may enter into **non-elect salvation**. They are saved **not by works alone**, but through Christ's mercy extended to those who practice charity and justice without knowing the full revelation of the gospel.

In **Chiliasm prophecy**, this event occurs at the **last trumpet**, the final resurrection at the end of the 1,000-year reign. By that time, the elect will have already been saved and glorified. The salvation of the "surprised sheep" thus happens **after** the millennial kingdom, reinforcing the idea that their salvation is **distinct in timing and nature** from that of the elect. They are raised in **terrestrial bodies**, destined for the new earth, while the elect, transformed at the end of the millennium, dwell in the new heavens in **celestial glory**.

Even **St. Irenaeus of Lyons** affirms this sequence. He writes that the elect are raised at the beginning of Christ's reign, which he calls the "times of the kingdom," while a second group of righteous is saved only at the **final judgment**, which he calls "after the times of the kingdom." This latter group corresponds to what he identifies as the **general resurrection**—in which the whole human race is judged, and some among them are separated as sheep, based not on faith but on righteousness in conduct.

In sum, rabbinical Judaism's distinction between **full** and **limited** proselytes mirrors, in a shadow form, the biblical and patristic distinction between **elect salvation** and **non-elect salvation**. The former involves full participation in the covenant and heavenly inheritance; the latter reflects God's gracious inclusion of the righteous among the nations—those who, though outside the Church, fulfill his moral law and show mercy to his people.

2.11 Sheep of the Other Fold

The expression **"sheep of the other fold"** found in John 10:16 has long been interpreted by many Church Fathers as referring to **Gentile believers** who would later be united with the Jewish flock through the gospel. While this interpretation gained popularity in later patristic writings, it is notably **absent** from the works of **Chiliasm Church Fathers** such as **St. Justin Martyr** and **St. Irenaeus of Lyons**—figures often valued for their proximity to apostolic teaching.

Instead, Irenaeus appears to present a more complex vision, one that may involve **two groups of sheep saved at different times**, separated by 1,000 years. The first group participates in the **first resurrection** during the "times of the kingdom"—the millennial reign of Christ—and is associated with **elect salvation**. The second group arises in the **general resurrection** at the **last trumpet**—a separate event which Irenaeus calls "after the times of the kingdom." This latter group could correspond to the **non-elect sheep**, possibly identified as the "sheep of the other fold".

In the writings of both **Justin Martyr** and **Irenaeus**, these non-Jewish sheep are not described using the term "other fold" but rather as **"spotted" or "colored sheep."** These descriptors emphasize **external distinctions**, such as ethnicity or outward difference, rather than internal covenant identity. By contrast, the Greek word for "fold" (αὐλῆς, *aulēs*) refers not to the sheep themselves but to their **dwelling place**—a sheep pen or enclosure. Thus, the distinction is not physical or racial, but **geographical or positional**: the elect sheep belong to the heavenly fold—the **New Jerusalem**—while the non-elect sheep may be assigned to the **new earth**, outside the city's gates, yet still within God's kingdom.

Early sources such as **Clement of Alexandria** also suggest that the "sheep of the other fold" could refer to individuals who undergo postmortem judgment and are placed in a **lesser final estate**. Some in Catholic tradition have seen in this the roots of purgatorial thought. However, it may also support the broader framework of **non-elect salvation**, especially for those who respond to truth **after death**, as implied in certain passages from early texts.

A particularly rich source is a difficult quote from **Irenaeus**, in which he refers to a group of "lost sheep" whom the Savior came to retrieve and transfer to the right hand—those who were not destroyed, but were **of the fold** and **of the left hand**. Irenaeus criticizes the Gnostics for using this image to build a numerological theory that fails to complete the full number of 100 sheep. He warns that the "enjoyment of rest" alone does not imply salvation. Yet, even this critique implies that some of these sheep do find rest and are **transferred** to the right hand—echoing the imagery of **Matthew 25:31–46**, where Christ separates the sheep and the goats.

This act of **separating** sheep from goats at the **second resurrection** (after the 1,000-year reign) suggests that these sheep—though not among the glorified elect—are still **saved by judgment**, not excluded from God's mercy. If correct, this aligns with the view that the "sheep of the other fold" represents a **distinct group saved postmortem**, not during the present age or the millennial kingdom, but **on Judgment Day itself.**

In this context, the **Apocalypse of Abraham**, a non-canonical Jewish writing, provides a similar vision: people on the **left side** of a divine image are judged, and some are transferred to the **right side** for restoration. While not inspired, such writings echo ancient traditions and offer insight into early Jewish-Christian expectations about post-judgment mercy.

Finally, one more statement by Irenaeus may further support this view. He distinguishes between **saved sheep of Israel** and **lost sheep**—the latter perhaps referring to those who are **not saved in this life**, but may be recovered later. He speaks of Christ descending to the **lower parts of the earth**, seeking the "sheep which had perished." This descending language refers not to earthly ministry, but to the **spirit world**—suggesting that some may be saved **after death**, though not as part of the Church Bride.

In summary, while later theology often limited the meaning of "other sheep" to Gentile converts, the earliest Chiliastic interpretation—especially through Irenaeus—opens up the possibility that Jesus was speaking of **a future group**, saved not through elect status, but through **divine mercy after judgment**. This group, resurrected alongside the wicked but separated out as righteous on that day, may represent the **non-elect sheep of the other fold.**

2.12 Indian Evidence – Sadhu Sundar Singh and D.G.S. Dhinakaran

Dr. D.G.S. Dhinakaran (1935–2008), founder of the *Jesus Calls* ministry, was one of India's most prominent evangelical preachers. Another towering figure in Indian Christianity was **Sadhu Sundar Singh** (1889–1929), whose life, writings, and mysterious disappearance into the Himalayas deeply influenced generations of Indian believers. Sundar Singh's conversion testimony is striking: after years of hostility toward Christianity—including burning a Bible and planning to end his life—he claimed that Christ appeared to him personally, resulting in a dramatic transformation of heart and calling.

What makes Sundar Singh particularly relevant to this study is his consistent claim to have witnessed **non-elect salvation** during spirit world visions. He recounted encounters in which individuals, including a sincere atheist and a Hindu idolater, were saved *after* experiencing judgment in the spirit realm. In these accounts, they came to acknowledge Christ and were eventually received into divine fellowship—not as glorified saints, but as those shown mercy through repentance after death.

One vision described a philosopher who had lived with moral conscience but without faith. Upon death, his spirit wandered in darkness, bumping about in confusion until repentance softened his heart. He then received instruction from angelic beings and was gradually brought into the light of God. Another account featured a devoted idol-worshiper who, upon realizing in the spirit world that there was only one true God and that Christ was his manifestation, sincerely repented. Christ appeared to him in dim light, and his errors were washed away. He and others like him were then welcomed with joy by saints appointed to guide such souls.

Sundar Singh also recorded that **Swedenborg**, the 18th-century mystic and theologian who advocated a form of non-elect salvation, appeared to him in these visions. Their conversations, he claimed, confirmed the reality of postmortem salvation for some souls. Swedenborg himself had written of meeting figures like **St. Augustine of Hippo** in the spirit world and held similar views about divine mercy extending beyond earthly life.

Despite these controversial claims, Dr. Dhinakaran testified that he personally encountered **Sundar Singh in heaven**. He wrote, *"There were occasions when the Lord enabled me to have some time in the Second Heaven with Sadhu Sundar Singh, the great and acclaimed Saint of India. The divine joy that was reflected on his face is beyond any description."* Dhinakaran's Pentecostal background didn't prevent him from affirming Sundar Singh's authenticity—even though Singh himself was not Pentecostal.

Many Pentecostals and Charismatics hold Dhinakaran's visions in high regard. If he truly saw Sundar Singh in heaven, then either Singh's views on non-elect salvation were **accurate**, or—if mistaken—such beliefs did not disqualify him from God's grace. This distinction is crucial: it implies that theological error on secondary eschatological matters does not necessarily imperil one's salvation, especially when the core of faith in Christ remains intact.

As the author notes, this section is not a dogmatic declaration but a **presentation of strong evidence**. While hopeful that non-elect salvation may prove true, the author remains neutral on matters that cannot be confirmed this side of eternity. In prophetic and visionary matters, he adopts a careful posture—arguing for the most probable case while clearly disclosing areas of uncertainty.

This approach finds precedent in **St. Justin Martyr**, who wrote that no believer enters heaven until the bodily resurrection, because the transition from "natural body" to "spiritual body" must occur for entrance into the final heavens. Justin did not deny that heavenly visions may occur, as in **2 Corinthians 12:2**, but he opposed teachings that claimed **disembodied spirit existence** in heaven apart from bodily resurrection. His perspective was shaped by the **Chiliasm tradition**, which maintained a physical resurrection of the saints before their glorified entrance into heaven.

Thus, Justin's stance does not conflict with Dhinakaran's or Singh's visions—if they are understood as **God-granted glimpses**, not permanent states of disembodied glory. Even Christ's own resurrection demonstrates this order: he did not ascend into heaven until after bodily resurrection. Likewise, believers await transformation before entering the final heavens.

Indian Christian testimony, especially from respected figures like **Sadhu Sundar Singh** and **D.G.S. Dhinakaran**, offers a unique cultural witness to the theological possibility of **non-elect salvation**. While these experiences are not scriptural in authority, they resonate with the broader pattern found in early Church writings and biblical prophecy—showing that God's mercy may be deeper and more expansive than traditional categories have allowed.

What if non-elect salvation turns out to be false?

The prophet **Jeremiah** warns that if someone speaks their own interpretation without claiming divine authority and it proves incorrect, the error is not necessarily damning. However, if someone falsely claims, "God told me so," and it turns out to be untrue, they are guilty of misusing the divine name and may incur **eternal shame or judgment**. The Hebrew term *olam*—often translated as "everlasting" or "perpetual"—appears twice in that context, underscoring the gravity of prophetic misrepresentation.

Yet what if **non-elect salvation** turns out to be true?

If it is, then Jesus' statement that "few" are saved may apply to **elect salvation**—those who become his **Bride** and enter **heaven**—while the "many" for whom Christ died may include others who, though not among the glorified saints, are still granted eternal life on the **new earth**. These are called by the Bride to take of the **water of life**, which flows freely into that final earthly kingdom. As **Revelation 22** describes, the **leaves of the tree of life** are given for the **healing of the nations**—possibly those saved by fire, yet not glorified.

Such individuals are not the Church, which is already resurrected and reigning for 1,000 years in the Chiliastic timeline. Thus, it would be difficult to imagine that the elect would need healing after glorification. Instead, it is more consistent with prophecy that the **"nations" outside the New Jerusalem**—described in Revelation 21:24–26—are the non-elect saved after judgment. **Daniel 12** may also support this, stating that *"many will be purified and made white and tried by fire"*—a possible reference to non-elect salvation through judgment.

This possibility could explain why some passages suggest that a larger group will be saved than is usually taught. Elect believers may be a subset of this greater multitude, differentiated by their inheritance and glory rather than their basic redemption.

The concept of non-elect salvation is not proposed here as a doctrine, but as an **academic hypothesis**. It cannot be affirmed with certainty, and therefore must be held **humbly and provisionally**. It is an interpretive possibility drawn directly from Scripture and Church history, intended to align with the **literal meaning of the biblical text**. As such, its inclusion is a scholarly exercise—not a demand for dogmatic affirmation.

To speak of prophecy responsibly, one must avoid **private interpretations**. That is why this work draws extensively on the writings of the **Chiliasm Church Fathers**, not modern speculation. Even if the interpretation proves inaccurate, the honesty of such investigation—rooted in historical sources—should not bring reproach. God does not condemn sincere efforts made with reverence and scholarly care, especially when they are submitted as possibilities, not as presumptuous claims.

Thus, non-elect salvation stands not as a rival gospel, but as a possible framework to reconcile God's justice with his mercy. Whether in the **spirit world**, during the **second resurrection**, or in the **final restoration**, the hope remains that **Christ's atonement** reaches further than traditionally assumed—saving not only the elect Bride, but also calling to others, saying:

"Come! And let the one who hears say, 'Come!' And let the one who is thirsty come. Let the one who wishes take the water of life without cost." (Revelation 22:17)

CHAPTER 2 The 1000-Year Divide: Prophecy and the Two Resurrections

Introduction

This essay presents original research into a topic rarely discussed among theologians and Bible scholars: the possibility that **1 Thessalonians 4:17** and **1 Corinthians 15:52** describe **two distinct prophetic events** separated by a span of **1,000 years**. Although many assume these verses both describe a single event—commonly referred to as the "rapture"—a close examination of **Chiliasm Church Fathers** reveals that they understood these texts very differently.

The passages in question read as follows:

"Then we who are alive and remain shall be caught up together with them in the clouds to meet the Lord in the air. And so we shall always be with the Lord." (1 Thessalonians 4:17)

"Now this I say, brethren, that flesh and blood cannot inherit the kingdom of God, nor does corruption inherit incorruption. Behold, I tell you a mystery: We shall not all sleep, but we shall all be changed—in a moment, in the twinkling of an eye, at the last trumpet. For the trumpet will sound, and the dead will be raised incorruptible, and we shall be changed." (1 Corinthians 15:50–52)

In standard Christian eschatology—whether **pre-tribulation, mid-tribulation,** or **post-tribulation**—these two verses are almost universally interpreted as referring to the **same future resurrection event**. This interpretation assumes that the "trumpet" mentioned in both passages is one and the same, heralding the transformation of the saints and their gathering to Christ. But what if this assumption is incorrect?

In this essay, we will explore a literal prophetic framework rooted in **Chiliasm**—the early Christian belief in a **1,000-year reign of Christ on earth** following his second coming. According to this view, 1 Thessalonians 4:17 refers to the **first resurrection**, which occurs at the **second coming of**

Christ, when believers are raised in **sinless human bodies** to reign with Christ on earth. Meanwhile, 1 Corinthians 15:52 refers to a **second and final transformation**—into **angelic, celestial bodies**—which takes place **after** the 1,000 years, at the **general resurrection** and **final judgment**.

This approach may be described as a kind of **prophetic archaeology**— a rediscovery of interpretive insights that were once held by the early Church but later lost or forgotten. The Church Fathers who held to Chiliasm— including **Tertullian, Victorinus, Methodius,** and **Irenaeus**—offer a consistent and compelling testimony that supports this view. Their writings reveal a structured, two-phase eschatology: first, a terrestrial resurrection for reigning on the earth, and later, a celestial transformation for eternal life in the new heavens.

If this distinction proves valid, it not only reshapes our understanding of the end times, but also helps resolve tensions in the biblical timeline. It accounts for the **two resurrections** described in Revelation 20, the **two trumpet calls**, and the **two stages of glorification**—human and then angelic. It also helps us distinguish between the **current heavens and earth**, which are still accessible to sin, and the **new heavens and new earth**, which are entirely incorruptible (Revelation 21:1).

The implications are significant: what many have merged into one event may in fact be **two prophetic milestones**, separated by **a literal millennium**. This essay will evaluate both texts carefully in their biblical and historical contexts, assess the testimony of the Church Fathers, and address objections to the Chiliasm framework.

In doing so, we hope to recover a forgotten key to eschatological clarity—and offer a humble invitation to reconsider what Scripture may be saying more plainly than we have previously understood.

PAPIAS OF HIERAPOLIS

Who was Papias?

Papias of Hierapolis (c. 60–163 C.E.) was one of the earliest post-apostolic Church Fathers, known for preserving apostolic teaching through oral tradition. A hearer of **John the Apostle** and a companion of **Polycarp**, Papias is often cited by **Irenaeus** and **Eusebius** as a trustworthy witness to early Christian doctrine. Though much of his work survives only in fragments, his statements regarding the resurrection and millennial reign carry considerable theological weight.

Papias is perhaps the earliest recorded proponent of **Chiliasm**—the view that Christ will return to establish a **literal 1,000-year reign** on earth, during which the faithful will be raised and rewarded in human form before the final glorification into heavenly, incorruptible existence.

One of the most telling fragments attributed to Papias describes a **three-tiered structure of the final state of the saved**, based on the parable of the Sower and the teaching of Jesus in John 14:2. He writes:

> "As the presbyters say, then those who are deemed worthy of an abode in heaven shall go there, others shall enjoy the delights of Paradise, and others shall possess the splendour of the city; for everywhere the Saviour will be seen, according as they shall be worthy who see Him. But that there is this distinction between the habitation of those who produce a hundredfold, and that of those who produce sixtyfold, and that of those who produce thirtyfold; for the first will be taken up into the heavens, the second class will dwell in Paradise, and the last will inhabit the city; and that on this account the Lord said, 'In my Father's house are many mansions'" (John 14:2).

This passage suggests that all three groups—the hundredfold, sixtyfold, and thirtyfold—will be saved, but each will inherit a **different level of reward and proximity to Christ**. The heavenly abode, Paradise, and the New Jerusalem city represent ascending degrees of blessedness. Importantly, this reflects a **gradational model of glorification**, wherein believers receive differing inheritances based on their spiritual fruitfulness.

Before presenting Papias's quote, the author of this essay rightly notes the limited biblical data concerning multiple **"heavens"**. The Apostle Paul speaks of the "third heaven" in 2 Corinthians 12:2, identifying it as **Paradise**. Some Jewish traditions likewise describe multiple heavenly realms, suggesting a framework that distinguishes between **heavenly layers** or domains. Papias appears to draw upon this background when describing believers' final destinations.

Irenaeus, who held Papias in high regard, confirms this tiered view of the afterlife and affirms its alignment with apostolic teaching. According to this framework, the **New Jerusalem**—which descends from heaven in Revelation 21—is likely the lowest tier of the heavenly kingdom. It serves as the final home of the "thirtyfold" reward group and may represent a shared gathering place for all the saved, though not all experience the same degree of proximity to God's glory.

This structure also supports the broader **Chiliasm timeline** upheld in this essay. The saints are resurrected into **sinless, natural human bodies** at the return of Christ (1 Thessalonians 4:17) to reign during the millennium. After the **1,000 years**, they are glorified into **angelic, celestial bodies** at the final judgment (1 Corinthians 15:52). Papias's gradation model implies that the **ultimate glorification**—being taken into the highest heavens—is a reward for those who produced the greatest spiritual fruit, consistent with the doctrine of **varying degrees of reward** in eternity.

Moreover, Papias describes this final arrangement as the "couch" at which the saved will recline during the marriage supper of the Lamb. This imagery echoes Revelation 19 and Christ's own parables about banquet invitations, further affirming a literal and ordered fulfillment of salvation history.

In summary, Papias provides **early and powerful support** for a **two-phase eschatology**:

1. **Resurrection and millennial reign** in glorified human form (earthly rule).

2. **Final glorification and translation** into distinct heavenly domains, based on reward and spiritual maturity.

His testimony predates that of many Church Fathers and carries unique credibility due to his direct connection to the apostolic circle. As such, Papias's vision affirms that **1 Thessalonians 4:17** and **1 Corinthians 15:52** describe **two separate prophetic milestones**, separated by a **literal millennium** and culminating in a divinely ordered hierarchy of eternal reward.

SHEPHERD OF HERMAS

Among early Christian writings, **The Shepherd of Hermas** holds a unique position. Though not part of the canon for most Christian traditions today, it was considered **Scripture or near-Scripture** by several early Church Fathers. These include Chiliast Fathers such as **Irenaeus of Lyons** and even **Tertullian**, who both regarded it with deep theological respect. The *Shepherd* was included in several early biblical collections, such as the **Muratorian Canon** in the West and the **Codex Sinaiticus** in the East.

In fact, **Irenaeus** quoted it as "Scripture," demonstrating its high authority in early Christian theology:

"Truly, then, the Scripture declared, which says, 'First of all believe that there is one God, who has established all things...'"

This quotation aligns with a preserved portion of *The Shepherd*, affirming its early acceptance as inspired or semi-inspired text.

The **Muratorian Fragment**, dated to around 170 C.E., acknowledges that Hermas wrote *The Shepherd* during the time of his brother Pius, bishop of Rome. Although it could not be read in the churches as canonical Scripture, the text affirms it was still **valuable for private reading and edification**:

"Therefore, it ought indeed to be read; but it cannot be read publicly to the people in church either among the Prophets... or among the Apostles, for it is after their time."

Even **St. Athanasius the Great**, who formally listed the 27 books of the New Testament, did not condemn the *Shepherd*—in fact, he placed it on the same level as **Esther**, a book still included in Protestant Bibles today.

Theologically, the *Shepherd* portrays **elect salvation** through the image of a **Tower of Repentance**, representing the Church. In one of its parables, the Church is described as a tower under construction, and people are symbolized as stones being examined for placement:

"The tower which you see building is myself, the Church… Ask, then, whatever you like in regard to the tower, and I will reveal it to you, that you may rejoice with the saints."

This "elect tower" represents those who are counted among the righteous, the Church's members who live in repentance and obedience.

Yet what is especially relevant to this essay is the *Shepherd's* treatment of **non-elect salvation**. It uniquely suggests that there may be **salvation outside the tower**, in a place of lesser glory, reserved for those who once heard the Gospel and even desired baptism—but did not follow through or fell into persistent sin. The vision says:

"Do you wish to know who are the others which fell near the waters, but could not be rolled into them? These are they who have heard the word and wish to be baptized... but again walk after their own wicked desires."

When asked whether these "rejected stones" can still be saved, the angel responds:

"Repentance is yet possible, but in this tower they cannot find a suitable place. But in another and much inferior place they will be laid... only when they have been tortured and completed the days of their sins. And on this account will they be transferred, because they have partaken of the righteous Word."

This suggests a form of **post-judgment salvation**, but distinct from the **glory and status of the elect**. Their salvation is conditional upon repentance through a time of suffering or chastisement—a concept resembling, but not identical to, later **Catholic purgatory**. Crucially, the *Shepherd* says that these individuals will not be placed in the tower but in another place altogether.

This passage also contributes to the **non-elect salvation model** explored throughout this essay. The "tower" may symbolize the elect dwelling in the **new heavens**, while those placed outside—after judgment and purifying correction—may represent the **non-elect redeemed** who inherit a place in the **new earth**, apart from the highest glory but nevertheless saved.

Even **Tertullian**, though cautious about some of the *Shepherd's* implications, affirmed the authenticity of this text. He acknowledged that while it was not accepted into the official canon due to its date of authorship, its message could not be easily dismissed. He wrote:

"I, however, imbibe the Scriptures of that Shepherd who cannot be broken."

Thus, while Tertullian wrestled with the implications of its generous offer of posthumous mercy, he still treated it as a serious theological source—especially when it came to describing a category of salvation that falls short of election, yet avoids destruction.

In summary, the **Shepherd of Hermas** offers a unique witness to early Christian views of both **elect and non-elect salvation**. It affirms the first resurrection and glorification of the saints but leaves open a second, lower-tiered hope for those who failed to enter the Church's tower yet partook of Christ's Word. This fits seamlessly into the broader framework of **a millennial gap between two resurrections and two types of final inheritance**—glory for the elect, and mercy for the repentant among the non-elect.

JUSTIN OF ROME

Who was Justin?

Let us begin with **Justin of Rome** (also known as **Justin Martyr**, c. 100–160 C.E.), one of the most influential early Christian apologists. Also referred to as **Justin of Neapolis**, he is recognized across multiple Christian traditions—including Catholicism, Orthodoxy, Anglicanism, and Lutheranism—as both a saint and martyr. A strong proponent of **Chiliasm**, Justin affirmed a literal 1,000-year reign of Christ on earth, aligning him with the earliest eschatological framework of the Church. He remains an authoritative voice in both theological philosophy and biblical interpretation.

Justin clearly affirms that there are only **two public comings of Christ**: the first in humility and suffering, and the second in glory and judgment. There is **no reference to a secret or pre-tribulation rapture** of the faithful prior to the rise of the Antichrist. Instead, Justin asserts that Christ's second coming occurs **after the man of lawlessness** is revealed and begins to persecute Christians—a context that aligns with **1 Thessalonians 4:17**, not with a pre-tribulational escape.

In *Dialogue with Trypho*, Justin writes:

> "O unreasoning men! Understanding not what has been proved by all these passages, that two advents of Christ have been announced: the one, in which he is set forth as suffering, inglorious, dishonoured, and crucified; but the other, in which he shall come from heaven with glory, when the man of apostasy, who speaks strange things against the Most High, shall venture to do unlawful deeds on the earth against us, the Christians... For the prophets have proclaimed two advents of his: the one, that which is already past, when he came as a dishonoured and suffering man; but the second, when, according to prophecy, he shall come from heaven with glory, accompanied by his angelic host, when also he shall raise the bodies of all men who have lived, and shall clothe those of the worthy with immortality, and shall send those of the wicked, endued with eternal sensibility, into everlasting fire with the wicked devils".

Some may read this statement and assume that Justin believed in a **single resurrection event**—one in which both the righteous and the wicked are raised at the same time. However, this would be a misreading. The above passage is a **summary** statement, not a detailed chronology. Elsewhere in his writings, Justin clearly affirms a **literal 1,000-year reign** of Christ **preceding the general resurrection and judgment**.

In another portion of the *Dialogue with Trypho*, Justin writes:

"But I and others, who are right-minded Christians on all points, are assured that there will be a resurrection of the dead, and a thousand years in Jerusalem, which will then be built, adorned, and enlarged, [as] the prophets Ezekiel and Isaiah and others declare... And further, there was a certain man with us, whose name was John, one of the apostles of Christ, who prophesied by a revelation that was made to him, that those who believed in our Christ would dwell a thousand years in Jerusalem; and that thereafter the general, and, in short, the eternal resurrection and judgment of all men would likewise take place".

This passage outlines a **clear two-phase resurrection sequence**:

1. The **first resurrection**, reserved for the elect, who are raised to reign with Christ in a restored Jerusalem for 1,000 years.

2. The **general resurrection**, which follows the millennium, includes both the righteous who were not part of the first resurrection and the wicked who are judged and condemned.

This framework is consistent with Revelation 20:4–6, which speaks of a **first resurrection** and a **second death**. Justin's language reflects this scriptural sequence—those who participate in the first resurrection are **blessed and holy**, while the rest of the dead **do not live again until the thousand years are finished.**

Thus, in Justin's theology, **1 Thessalonians 4:17** refers to the first resurrection, when believers meet Christ at his second coming to begin the millennial reign. Meanwhile, **1 Corinthians 15:52**—where Paul speaks of a transformation "at the last trumpet"—refers to the **final change** that occurs after the 1,000 years, when mortality is fully swallowed up in immortality. This harmonizes with other Chiliastic Fathers and provides strong textual support for a **1,000-year prophetic gap** between these two verses.

Justin Martyr's testimony serves as a foundation for this interpretive model. He presents an eschatology that is both **biblical and early**, rooted not in speculation but in apostolic tradition. Far from being a fringe idea, this distinction between two stages of resurrection and glorification was once **mainstream in early Christianity**. Rediscovering it today may help restore theological precision to the Church's understanding of prophecy.

IRENAEUS OF LYONS

Who was Irenaeus?

St. Irenaeus of Lyons (c. 130–202 C.E.) was a pivotal early Church Father and theologian, widely respected for preserving and defending apostolic doctrine. A disciple of **Polycarp**, who himself was taught by the apostle John, Irenaeus forms a critical link between the New Testament Church and the second century. His theological masterpiece, *Against Heresies*, refutes Gnostic distortions and sets forth a robust defense of orthodox Christian eschatology, including a literal 1,000-year reign of Christ on earth. Among the early proponents of **Chiliasm**, Irenaeus stands out for his detailed and structured understanding of the resurrection and glorification of the saints.

In Book 5 of *Against Heresies*, Irenaeus affirms a **two-stage post-resurrection transformation**. First, the righteous are raised to reign with Christ during the millennium. Then, after the final judgment and the destruction of the current heavens and earth, the faithful are translated into the **eternal kingdom of heaven**. He writes:

> "For it was necessary, at first, that nature should be exhibited; then, after that, that what was mortal should be conquered and swallowed up by immortality, and the corruptible by incorruptibility, and that man should be made after the image and likeness of God, having received the knowledge of good and evil."

This aligns with Paul's teaching in **1 Corinthians 15:52**, where believers are *"changed in a moment, in the twinkling of an eye"*—a transformation Irenaeus places **after the millennium**, when the righteous inherit their **celestial, incorruptible bodies**.

Irenaeus elaborates further:

> "These are inherited by the Spirit when they are translated into the kingdom of heaven. For this cause, too, did Christ die, that the Gospel covenant... might in the first place set free his slaves; and then afterward... constitute them heirs of his property, when the Spirit possesses them by inheritance."

He explains that *flesh and blood cannot inherit the kingdom of God*—a phrase taken directly from **1 Corinthians 15:50**—and warns that without the indwelling Spirit, believers remain "mere flesh and blood" and thus unfit for the final kingdom. In this model, the elect are first raised in **sinless natural bodies** to reign on earth (the millennium), and then transformed into **spiritual bodies** to inherit the new heavens.

This sequence is not allegorical. Irenaeus describes the Church as a *"beautiful elect tower"* being built across the earth—a parabolic image also found in the **Shepherd of Hermas**, a text he considered scriptural. The elect participate in the **first resurrection**, reign during the 1,000 years, and are only afterwards glorified with full heavenly inheritance.

He writes:

> "The living inherit, but the flesh is inherited… unless the Word of God dwell with, and the Spirit of the Father be in you… you cannot inherit the kingdom of God."

This parallels Revelation 21, where the **Bride descends from heaven** after the millennium—suggesting the glorification described in **1 Corinthians 15:52** occurs at that moment, not before.

For Irenaeus, then, the **resurrection** at Christ's return is **not yet glorification**. It is a stage of restoration into sinless humanity, still distinct from the final, angelic state. The full "change" comes **later**, in a second transformation when "mortality is swallowed up by life."

This reading reinforces the position that **1 Thessalonians 4:17** describes the **first resurrection**—a return to bodily life for the saints to reign with Christ—while **1 Corinthians 15:52** describes the **final glorification** into spiritual bodies fit for heaven, which occurs after the **millennial reign** and **final judgment**.

In Irenaeus's theology, as in the broader Chiliasm tradition, this two-phase hope offers a majestic vision of God's redemptive order: first, a purified earth under Christ's rule; then, an eternal, incorruptible cosmos in which the righteous dwell in full divine glory.

TERTULLIAN

Who was Tertullian?

Tertullian (c. 155–240 C.E.) is widely regarded as the **father of Latin Christianity** and a foundational figure in the development of **Western theological thought**. He was an ardent proponent of **Chiliasm**, the belief in a literal 1,000-year reign of Christ on earth following his second coming. Alongside Irenaeus of Lyons and Justin of Rome, Tertullian represents the earliest generation of post-apostolic Christian thinkers whose writings contain significant theological depth. While Tertullian is not recognized as a saint by the Roman Catholic Church—largely due to his later association with **Montanism**—his contributions to Christian doctrine remain substantial and influential.

Tertullian, like Justin, affirmed **only two comings of Christ**: the first in humility, already fulfilled, and the second in unveiled majesty and judgment. He writes:

> "For two comings of Christ have been revealed to us: a first, which has been fulfilled in the lowliness of a human lot; a second, which impends over the world, now near its close, in all the majesty of Deity unveiled; and, by misunderstanding the first, they have concluded that the second—which, as matter of more manifest prediction, they set their hopes on—is the only one." (*Against Marcion*, Book 3, Chapter 25).

There is no suggestion in Tertullian's writings of a secret rapture or a pre-tribulation removal of the Church. On the contrary, he affirms a **post-tribulational gathering** of the saints at Christ's visible return, after the final Antichrist has come. Regarding **1 Thessalonians 4:17**, he interprets it as describing the resurrection and transformation of believers **at the time of Christ's return following tribulation**:

> "Now the privilege of this favour awaits those who shall at the coming of the Lord be found in the flesh, and who shall, owing to the oppressions of the time of Antichrist, deserve by an instantaneous death, which is accomplished by a sudden change, to become qualified to join the rising saints..." (*On the Resurrection of the Flesh*, Chapter 42).

Tertullian's reading of **1 Corinthians 15:52**, however, places that "change in the twinkling of an eye" **after the 1,000-year reign**, at the end of history. He writes one of the clearest distinctions found in early Christian literature:

> "Of the heavenly kingdom this is the process. After its thousand years are over, within which period is completed the resurrection of the saints... there will ensue the destruction of the world and the conflagration of all things at the judgment: we shall then be changed in a moment into the substance of angels, even by the investiture of an incorruptible nature, and so be removed to that kingdom in heaven... But the resurrection is one thing, and the kingdom is another. The resurrection is first, and afterwards the kingdom." (*Against Marcion*, Book 5, Chapter 10).

This remarkable passage confirms the **two-stage eschatological structure** found in earlier writings:

1. The **first resurrection**—associated with 1 Thessalonians 4:17—occurs at the beginning of the millennium. Believers are raised into **sinless, natural human bodies** to reign with Christ on earth.

2. The **final transformation**—linked to 1 Corinthians 15:52—occurs after the millennium, when these believers are changed into **angelic, incorruptible beings** to dwell eternally in the heavenly kingdom.

Tertullian therefore distinguishes between **resurrection** and **transformation** as two separate prophetic events, separated by **1,000 years**. This aligns precisely with the vision presented in Revelation 20, which describes the **first resurrection** of the saints, followed by a long reign, and finally the **judgment of the rest of the dead**.

Importantly, Tertullian does not equate being raised from the dead with immediate glorification. He sees resurrection as the **first step**, not the culmination. Only after the full thousand years does the **substance of angels**—a celestial body suitable for heaven—become the inheritance of the saints. He makes a clear distinction: *"The resurrection is first, and afterwards the kingdom."* This "kingdom" refers to the **eternal heavenly realm**, not the millennial reign on earth.

In summary, Tertullian strengthens the claim that **1 Thessalonians 4:17** and **1 Corinthians 15:52** describe **two distinct stages** in God's redemptive timeline, with **a literal millennium between them**. His voice joins Justin and Irenaeus in establishing a pattern long ignored in modern eschatology but deeply rooted in the earliest Christian testimony.

VICTORINUS

Who was Victorinus?

Victorinus of Pettau (also spelled Poetovio, modern-day Ptuj, Slovenia) was an early Christian bishop and martyr who lived during the third century and died around 304 C.E. during the Diocletian persecution. He was the **first Latin commentator on the Book of Revelation**, and his eschatological writings reflect a robust Chiliasm—an interpretive tradition rooted in a literal understanding of the 1,000-year reign of Christ. His works are among the earliest extant commentaries on the Apocalypse.

Victorinus makes a crucial distinction between the **trumpet** in **1 Thessalonians 4:17** and the "last trumpet" mentioned in **1 Corinthians 15:52**. In his view, the trumpet of Thessalonians pertains to **Christ's return to establish his millennial kingdom**, whereas the trumpet in Corinthians points to a future moment **after the thousand years**, when the current heavens and earth will be destroyed and the saints fully glorified.

In his *Commentary on Revelation*, Victorinus writes:

> "The seventh trumpet is the last, after which there is no more trumpet... The trumpet shall sound, and the dead shall rise incorruptible, and we shall be changed. This is the last trumpet, of which Paul spoke. He did not say that we shall rise immortal, but we shall be changed."

This statement is significant. Victorinus emphasizes that believers are not **raised immortal** at the first resurrection but are instead **changed later**—after the final trumpet, which he connects to the events following the millennium. This affirms a **two-stage glorification**: first, a resurrection into purified, natural human bodies for reigning on the earth; second, a transformation into angelic, celestial bodies fit for the eternal kingdom.

In the same commentary, Victorinus further notes:

> "This kingdom of the saints, spoken of, is the thousand years of earthly reign, after which comes the end of the world... and only then will the saints be glorified fully."

This mirrors the order found in Revelation 20–21, where the **first resurrection** precedes the **1,000-year reign**, followed by the **great white throne judgment**, the **second resurrection**, and finally the **new heavens and new earth**.

In other words, **1 Thessalonians 4:17** corresponds to the **first resurrection** and the beginning of the millennial reign, while **1 Corinthians 15:52** aligns with the **final trumpet**—sounding after the millennium—when believers are changed "in the twinkling of an eye" into their **incorruptible form**.

Victorinus thus supports the same two-phase prophetic framework affirmed by **Justin, Irenaeus,** and **Tertullian.** His interpretation reinforces the idea that **resurrection and glorification are not the same moment** but rather separated by the **millennial reign of Christ**.

His contribution is critical, as it shows continuity of this teaching into the late third century—a time when theological battles over resurrection, soul immortality, and eschatology were intensifying. Victorinus stood firm with the early fathers in his commitment to a **literal and structured prophetic timeline**, upholding a hope that is both earthly and heavenly, human and divine, staged and fulfilled.

METHODIUS OF OLYMPUS

Who was Methodius?

Methodius of Olympus (d. c. 311 C.E.) was a bishop, theologian, and Christian martyr who lived during the time of the Diocletian persecution. Though much of his work has been lost, two of his important surviving writings—*Banquet of the Ten Virgins* and *On the Resurrection*—highlight his commitment to **Chiliasm**, the belief in a literal 1,000-year reign of Christ on earth. He is remembered as a defender of **free will** against the fatalism of Gnostic thought and as a critic of certain Origenist teachings, particularly those concerning the nature of the resurrection.

Methodius explicitly taught that **1 Thessalonians 4:17** refers to the **rapture at the beginning of the millennium**, when the festival of the first resurrection commences. In his own words:

> "Those are our bodies; for the souls are we ourselves, who, rising, resume that which is dead from the earth; so that being caught up with them to meet the Lord, we may gloriously celebrate the splendid festival of the resurrection, because we have received our everlasting tabernacles, which shall no longer die nor be dissolved".

This affirms that believers receive **resurrected human bodies** at Christ's return—sinless, incorruptible, but still of earthly substance—so they may reign with Christ during the **millennial rest**.

However, Methodius also taught that **1 Corinthians 15:52** describes a **second transformation** that occurs **after the 1,000 years**, not at the same time as the first resurrection. He describes this change as the final translation of the saints into an **angelic, heavenly form**, fit not merely for earthly rule but for eternal inheritance. He writes:

> "Then again from thence I, a follower of Jesus, who has entered into the heavens... after the rest of the Feast of Tabernacles, came into the land of promise, come into the heavens, not continuing to remain in tabernacles—that is, my body not remaining as it was before, but, after the space of a thousand years, changed from a human and corruptible form into angelic size and beauty, where at last we virgins, when the festival of the resurrection is consummated, shall pass from the wonderful place of the tabernacle to greater and better things".

In this vision, Methodius draws upon the typology of the **Feast of Tabernacles**, portraying the millennium as a period of temporary dwelling in glorified human bodies—sinless but not yet heavenly. Only after this "seventh day," the true Sabbath of rest, are the saints changed "from a human and corruptible form into angelic size and beauty."

Methodius reinforces the distinction between the **two prophetic events** under examination. He identifies:

- **1 Thessalonians 4:17** with the **first resurrection**, at the start of the millennium.

- **1 Corinthians 15:52** with the **final transformation**, after the millennium has ended, when the **second resurrection** and final judgment unfold.

This teaching aligns with the views of **Tertullian** and **Irenaeus**, both of whom insist that the righteous must receive recompense **in the same creation in which they suffered**. In other words, the faithful are resurrected into earthly but sinless bodies in order to be rewarded **on earth** for their faithfulness—before being finally glorified with heavenly bodies fit for the **new creation**.

Methodius's view presents the eschatological timeline in two movements:

1. **Initial resurrection** into incorruptible but human form—fitting for the 1,000-year reign on earth.

2. **Final glorification** into angelic form—fitting for the eternal kingdom of heaven after the millennium.

This reinforces the proposition of a **literal 1,000-year gap** between the resurrection and the final change, as expressed in **1 Thessalonians 4:17** and **1 Corinthians 15:52** respectively.

In closing, Methodius offers profound theological insight consistent with early Christian Chiliasm. His clarity on the **two resurrections**, the **purpose of the millennial reign**, and the **final glorification** provides a vital witness to the structured nature of biblical prophecy—one that modern readers may do well to recover.

AUGUSTINE'S REJECTION OF CHILIASM

Who was Augustine?

St. Augustine of Hippo (354–430 C.E.) remains one of the most influential Christian theologians in history. His writings shaped the doctrines of both Western Catholicism and Protestantism. Known for theological masterpieces like *The City of God* and *Confessions*, Augustine eventually came to reject **Chiliasm**, the doctrine of a literal 1,000-year earthly reign of Christ—a view he originally held earlier in his Christian walk.

Yet what is not often acknowledged is the **significant influence of his teacher, St. Ambrose of Milan** (c. 340–397 C.E.), who baptized Augustine around 386 C.E. Ambrose held a **much broader view of salvation** than Augustine later did. One of Ambrose's statements illustrates this:

> "For now, since all do not believe, all do not seem to be in subjection. But when all have believed and done the will of God, then Christ will be all and in all. And when Christ is all and in all, then will God be all and in all."

This expansive hope impacted later Catholic thinking, particularly post-Vatican II, when the Catechism began emphasizing prayers for the salvation of "all men." Ambrose's openness to eventual universal reconciliation may have influenced Augustine's early thought before he shifted under the sway of **Origenist allegorization**.

Interestingly, Augustine did not regard **Christian Universalists**—those who believed in a temporal, purgatorial hell rather than an eternal one—as heretics. This is notable, as Church Fathers were often quick to condemn doctrinal deviations. Augustine even speculated about the **possibility of salvation outside the kingdom of God**, or what might be called **non-elect salvation** in the age to come. In one such reflection, he wrote that perhaps some may experience **"relief or intermission of their misery,"** suggesting gradations of post-judgment conditions rather than a blanket condemnation to eternal torment.

For today's readers, this opens the door to careful theological inquiry. If someone as revered as Augustine could explore such possibilities without incurring charges of heresy, then modern believers may likewise consider the **non-elect salvation model** as a possibility within orthodoxy—especially when based on early Church writings like those found in **Chiliasm**.

Even if Augustine ultimately rejected Chiliasm and embraced **amillennialism** (a symbolic view of the 1,000 years in Revelation 20), he remained a nuanced thinker. His movement away from literal interpretation was heavily influenced by **Origen of Alexandria**, who spiritualized nearly all eschatological prophecy. Nonetheless, Augustine preserved a reverence for earlier Church voices and traditions—even when he disagreed with them.

Therefore, in reflecting on Augustine's theological legacy, it is fair to say he **did not embrace Chiliasm**—but he also left space for **theological humility**. He modeled a posture of faithful inquiry, which suggests that proposing alternate views such as **a 1,000-year gap between the two prophetic transformations** (as found in 1 Thessalonians 4:17 and 1 Corinthians 15:52) is not irreverent or dangerous, but may be part of a broader rediscovery of lost interpretive clarity.

HOW DOES THIS COMPARE WITH OTHER BELIEFS AND RESEARCH?

In historical studies on chiliasm, it's often claimed that "other patriarchs excluded chiliasm." Yet, what's frequently left unsaid is that these same church fathers also **did not promote any allegorical interpretation** of the book of Revelation. Their actual stance on prophecy is thus unclear.

These same academic works often acknowledge that the strongest testimonies for chiliasm come from the **earliest church fathers**. Some critics claim these views were personal opinions rather than church-wide beliefs. However, such assertions are challenged by early sources like the *Didache*, widely accepted as a first-century Christian document. The *Didache* concludes with this statement:

> "And then shall appear the signs of the truth: first, the sign of an outspreading in heaven; then the sign of the sound of the trumpet; and third, the resurrection of the dead—yet not of all, but as it is said: 'The Lord shall come and all his saints with him.' Then shall the world see the Lord coming upon the clouds of heaven."

This early doctrinal stance plainly distinguishes between a **partial resurrection** (the righteous) and a general one. The phrase "yet not of all" strongly supports the concept of a **first resurrection**, which is a core teaching in chiliasm. In contrast, most allegorical interpretations teach only one resurrection for both the righteous and the wicked—occurring simultaneously at Christ's return.

This allegorical model has been widely adopted, especially by many **Reformation-era theologians**. The *Augsburg Confession*, a foundational document for Lutheranism, teaches this single-resurrection view as follows:

> "Also they teach that at the consummation of the world Christ will appear for judgment, and will raise up all the dead; he will give to the godly and elect eternal life and everlasting joys, but

ungodly men and the devils he will condemn to be tormented without end."

This clearly reflects the allegorical view: a **single judgment event**, rather than the **two-stage sequence** seen in the earliest Christian writings.

Importantly, **no early church fathers** from the apostolic or sub-apostolic periods support this allegorical view. It first appears in the works of **Origen of Alexandria** (c. 185–253) in the East and **Augustine of Hippo** (c. 354–430) in the West. Despite this relatively late emergence, many theologians mistakenly assume that the allegorical interpretation has roots in apostolic Christianity—when it does not.

A helpful theological principle emerges from this comparison: **any interpretation without clear patristic support should be approached with caution.** For example, **John Wesley** (1703–1791), the founder of Methodism, held a highly unusual eschatological position. He taught that after Christ's return, there would be **two consecutive millennia**, totaling **2,000 years** before the final judgment. No early church father taught such a view. It appears to be Wesley's personal speculation and, as such, carries little historical weight.

Likewise, **John Calvin** (1509–1564), father of Reformed theology, **rejected chiliasm** outright. He believed that emphasizing a literal 1,000-year reign diminished the glory of Christ's return. In *Institutes of the Christian Religion*, Calvin writes:

> "But Satan has not only befuddled men's senses to make them bury with the corpses the memory of resurrection; he has also attempted to corrupt this part of the doctrine with various falsifications that he might at length destroy it… but a little later there followed the chiliasts, who limited the kingdom to a thousand years… For if they do not put on immortality, then Christ himself, to whose glory they shall be transformed, has not been received into undying glory."

Calvin's concern was theological: that to delay immortality until after the millennium undermined the full glorification of Christ. However, this view overlooks that **many early church fathers** clearly taught a **first resurrection into human but sinless form**, followed by a **later glorification into heavenly bodies**—in no way denying Christ's glory.

In comparing chiliasm with these later doctrinal models, one truth becomes evident: the **earliest Christian writers consistently describe two distinct eschatological stages.** They affirm a resurrection at Christ's return for the saints, followed by a 1,000-year earthly reign, and then a final resurrection and transformation at the judgment. The allegorical and symbolic views emerged much later and appear **unsupported by patristic tradition** prior to the third century.

Thus, chiliasm is not a fringe theory but a well-attested belief held by many of the **first generations of Christians**, rooted in their interpretation of prophetic scripture and apostolic tradition. Any departure from this model—whether Origen's spiritualism or Calvin's doctrinal reaction—should be judged in light of what was believed **first**, not merely what became **popular later**.

Conclusion

Many Pentecostals today sincerely believe in the testimony of Dr. D.G.S. Dhinakaran, who claimed to have been to heaven and seen Sadhu Sundar Singh there. If such a vision were genuine, it would lend support to Sundar Singh's belief in the possibility of salvation for those outside the elect. Even if his views were mistaken, they have clearly not prevented many Christians and non-Christians alike from being deeply affected by them. This presents a significant theological challenge: either such claims are valid, or their inaccuracy does not threaten salvation.

For my part, I have presented the evidence supporting the possibility of non-elect salvation with conviction. I hope it proves true. Yet, I must admit that I cannot know with certainty until I die and stand before the Lord. I take a neutral position on matters that Scripture does not define with absolute clarity. However, in presenting the side that I believe is more likely based on Scripture and the writings of early Church Fathers, I aim to speak honestly without misleading others. By stating these possibilities up front, I ensure that no one is caught unaware by the speculative nature of some of these conclusions.

St. Justin Martyr wrote that no Christian enters heaven until after the resurrection, because we must be changed—transformed from our mortal, flesh-and-blood state to an immortal, spiritual body. Only then are we fit for heaven. This interpretation becomes clear when we consider the collective teaching of the early Church Fathers who affirmed Chiliasm. While Justin may not have stated everything explicitly, the broader context of his writing affirms this two-stage transformation. He was not denying the reality of divine visions (like that of Paul in 2 Corinthians 12:2), but was opposing the belief that people could permanently exist in heaven without a bodily resurrection.

This idea is reinforced by Jesus' own example. After his death, He did not go to heaven as a spirit. Instead, He waited until He was bodily resurrected. His resurrection body was not merely flesh and blood, but something glorified—beyond human nature. Similarly, those who are raised in the first resurrection do not yet share in the full transformation. That complete change comes after the millennial reign, when the "marriage of the Lamb" is fulfilled, and believers are made one flesh with Christ in glory.

Roman Catholics often appeal to Church Fathers like Irenaeus and Tertullian to argue that they possess an unbroken spiritual descent from the apostles. However, these same men also believed in Chiliasm—a literal 1,000-year reign of Christ on earth. If their words are to be used in support of Catholic continuity, then all of their theology, including their Chiliastic teachings, must be acknowledged. The fact that their writings contain elements no longer embraced by modern Catholic doctrine suggests that even the earliest churches allowed theological diversity. Dominant traditions were not always the result of divine revelation, but of human decision-making over time.

This mirrors what happened in Judaism. The Jews preserved the Scriptures, maintained a functioning Levitical priesthood, and welcomed converts for thousands of years. Yet by the time Christ came, many doctrinal errors had crept in—so much so that even with Scripture in hand, they failed to recognize the Messiah. This shows that doctrinal continuity does not guarantee doctrinal accuracy. Human free will plays a powerful role in shaping religious tradition.

Therefore, majority opinion—even among church leaders or councils—should not be mistaken for theological truth. In my view, the earliest Christian writings preserved by the Chiliastic Church Fathers—especially Irenaeus, Justin Martyr, and to some extent Tertullian—offer the most faithful account of apostolic teaching. Where they differ from one another, I tend to favor Irenaeus and Justin. Even Roman Catholic authorities acknowledge that Tertullian erred in several areas, which is one reason he was never canonized.

Consider also the testimony of Clement of Rome (c. 35–99 C.E.), known to Roman Catholics as Pope Clement I. He was a direct disciple of the apostle Peter. His letter, now known as 1 Clement, was considered Scripture by some early churches and is even included in Codex Alexandrinus from the fifth century. Irenaeus regarded this letter as an authentic apostolic tradition. In one passage, Clement describes how a person who separates from the church may still be more doctrinally accurate than the majority. This is an early affirmation of theological free will and a clear warning that even the consensus of a church body can be mistaken. God honors the one who stands for truth—even if they must stand alone.

So let us not be discouraged if we find ourselves holding to doctrines that are unpopular or rejected by the majority. Clement's statement should embolden all Christians to pursue doctrinal accuracy with humility and conviction. God does not measure our faithfulness by the size of our following but by our alignment with truth. Even in matters of prophecy, it is better to humbly pursue what seems true than to blindly follow the crowd.

This same principle applies to denominational growth. One might ask, "If God is sovereign, why do some denominations have more converts than others?" My belief is that God allows us to be led by the teachers we deserve. If more Christians were zealous for truth and precision in doctrine—as Irenaeus was—then God might raise up leaders who reflect that same spirit. Daniel's prophecy offers insight here. In Daniel 12:3, he writes that those who lead many to righteousness will shine like the stars. But those with insight—particularly in prophecy—will shine like the heavens themselves. This reflects different degrees of resurrection glory. Irenaeus himself affirmed that Daniel 12 refers to this final glorification based on prophetic and doctrinal understanding.

Therefore, we should strive not only to lead others to righteousness but also to gain insight and accuracy in doctrine. God will judge who shines like stars and who like the heavens. Jeremiah 23 warns us that if someone speaks presumptuously in God's name—saying "God told me" when He did not— they are guilty of misusing His name. But if one shares a possibility or opinion clearly marked as their own, even if it turns out wrong, they are not condemned. The Hebrew word *olam* (translated "everlasting" or "perpetual") is used twice in this warning, underscoring the seriousness of speaking falsely in God's name.

If the concept of non-elect salvation proves true, then the "few" who are saved refers to the elect—the Bride of Christ who inherits the heavenly kingdom. Meanwhile, the "many" who benefit from Christ's ransom could include the non-elect, who dwell on the new earth. Revelation 22 describes the Bride calling out to others to "take the water of life freely." This water flows into the new earth, and the tree of life provides healing to the nations. Since the elect are already glorified and reigning, it seems unlikely that they would need healing. This may suggest that those needing healing are the non-elect—those "saved by fire" (cf. 1 Corinthians 3:15).

Daniel 12:10 supports this: "Many shall be purified, made white, and refined." This process may describe salvation through fiery purification for those outside the elect. It would explain verses that hint at a large group being saved, even if only a few are the elect. In this view, believers are a subset of a broader class of redeemed individuals.

Even Jerome, translator of the Latin Vulgate, emphasized the importance of doctrinal precision using Daniel 12:3. Let us end with the Septuagint's rendering of this passage for comparison:

> "And many of them that sleep in the dust of the earth shall awake, some to everlasting life, and some to reproach and everlasting shame. And the wise shall shine as the brightness of the firmament, and some of the many righteous as the stars forever and ever... Many must be tested, and thoroughly whitened, and tried with fire, and sanctified; but the transgressors shall transgress, and none of the transgressors shall understand; but the wise shall understand" (Daniel 12:2–3,10, Brenton LXX).

If this understanding is correct—that Daniel 12 teaches varied levels of glory in the resurrection based on insight and faithfulness—then we should approach all doctrine, especially prophecy, with seriousness. The reward is not merely salvation but the measure of glory assigned to us in the resurrection. While leading many to righteousness brings glory like the stars, those who gain prophetic insight and doctrinal clarity will shine like the brightness of the heavens. This distinction is not metaphorical; it reflects the Chiliasm framework of layered glorification taught by the earliest post-apostolic Fathers.

The final judgment scene depicted in Revelation further supports the possibility of non-elect salvation. In Revelation 21, the New Jerusalem is revealed, and the nations are described as walking by its light (Revelation 21:24). The leaves of the tree of life are said to be "for the healing of the nations" (Revelation 22:2). These verses imply that there are people outside the Bride—the glorified Church—who are nonetheless granted life and healing. The righteous nations, who were not part of the first resurrection, are not condemned. They are not cast into the lake of fire. Instead, they are granted a form of post-judgment life on the new earth.

This fits the picture offered by the distinction between the elect and the non-elect. The elect are glorified, reign with Christ, and dwell in the New Jerusalem. The non-elect, by contrast, may be saved through fire, purified, and given life—but without entering the glorified city. They may dwell on the renewed earth, brought into peace and healing by the water and leaves that flow from the tree of life within the city. These individuals may correspond to the "many" who are purified, as Daniel prophesied, and to those described by Jesus in Matthew 25 as the "sheep" who cared for his brothers.

This model maintains fidelity to Scripture, affirms the reality of eternal judgment, upholds the necessity of Christ's atonement, and preserves the distinction between the Bride and the nations. It avoids the errors of universalism while allowing for a hopeful possibility: that God, in His mercy, may save some who are not part of the elect.

This entire vision is grounded not in modern innovation, but in the testimony of early Christian writers—especially those of the Chiliastic tradition. Their teachings have been overlooked or dismissed by allegorists and spiritualizers, but their clarity deserves a fresh hearing. If their view is right, then the "last trumpet" of 1 Corinthians 15:52 refers to a separate event from the trumpet in 1 Thessalonians 4:17. The first is for the elect—the Bride of Christ—at the start of the millennium. The last is for the final transformation after the millennial reign, when the dead are raised, and those deemed righteous among the nations are granted entry into life on the new earth.

If that is the case, the resurrection is not one event but a sequence: first the elect, then the non-elect. First the glorified Bride, then the nations healed by the tree of life. First those who reign with Christ, then those who receive mercy at His feet. This reading preserves the full breadth of biblical prophecy while maintaining the exclusivity of the Gospel and the supremacy of Christ's rule.

Let us be humble in doctrine, careful in prophecy, and bold in hope. For if even a portion of what has been explored here is true, then the love and justice of God are greater than we've dared to imagine—and His redemptive plan more intricate and merciful than most have taught.

Disclaimer

This article, titled *Non-Elect Salvation Possibility* (NESP), was recently published in *The American Journal of Biblical Theology*, Volume 26, Issue 6 (February 9, 2025). It is the author's first and only academic journal publication to date and spans fifty-two pages. The journal's publication policies allow authors to republish their work elsewhere, which is why this essay appears here in its revised form. The copyright of all published articles is retained by the author under Title 17 of the U.S. Code § 506. The journal maintains a fair use agreement to edit, format, and reproduce the author's work in any media it may publish in the future. However, the author remains free to republish the original manuscript in other journals as well.

CHAPTER 3 The Two Waters of Life: A Millennial Prophetic Gap?

Introduction

Scripture appears to present two distinct mentions of the "water of life" that are separated by a span of 1,000 years, in alignment with the Chiliasm timeline. According to this model, Christians—resurrected in sinless human bodies—receive the water of life at the beginning of the 1,000-year reign of Christ, which commences at His Second Coming during the First Resurrection. This initial fulfillment occurs on the current, yet renewed, old earth and in the present old heavens. Revelation 7:9–17 is widely understood to describe the multitude of Christians who are saved at Christ's return.

Mortals, or sinners, live alongside these resurrected Christian immortals during the millennial reign. This coexistence indicates that the setting must still be the old earth, for it can still be touched by sin. In contrast, the final new earth described in Revelation cannot be defiled by sin in any way. But doesn't Isaiah 65:17 speak of a "new heavens and a new earth," raising a question about this timing?

The answer lies in the context. Isaiah's prophecy refers not to the final new heavens and new earth but rather to a renewed version of the old earth. Revelation 21:1–3 makes this distinction clear. Justin Martyr (also called Justin of Rome) supports this interpretation when he quotes Isaiah 65:17 and states:

"But I and others, who are right-minded Christians on all points, are assured that there will be a resurrection of the dead, and a thousand years in Jerusalem, which will then be built, adorned, and enlarged, the prophets Ezekiel and Isaiah and others declare. For Isaiah spake thus concerning this space of a thousand years: 'For there shall be the new heaven and the new earth, and the former shall not be remembered, or come into their heart; but they shall find joy and gladness in it, which things I create.'"

This renewed earth during the Millennial Reign is described as still containing a literal "sea" (Ezekiel 47:7–12), while the final new earth has no sea at all (Revelation 21:1). Likewise, the "tree of life" seems to exist in two phases: first as a figure or type during the millennium, and later in its literal form on the final new earth. The variations within the descriptions of these events point to two separate stages—one allegorical and one literal—divided by the 1,000-year period, as affirmed in Chiliasm.

At the close of the 1,000 years, after the final judgment, some non-Christians may be invited to partake of the water of life. Revelation 22:17 describes this scene in which the "Bride"—meaning the glorified elect—is shown calling others to come. These others would therefore be distinct from the elect, possibly referring to the non-elect who are now granted salvation. This takes place after Judgment Day, on the final new earth and under the new heavens, as the results from the Book of Life have already been disclosed.

Scripture distinguishes between these groups:

i) Elect Salvation — those referred to as the "Bride," having participated in the First Resurrection and the Marriage of the Lamb (compare with Matthew 25:1–13).

> "And the Spirit and the bride say, 'Come!'" (Revelation 22:17)

ii) Non-Elect Salvation for Israel — identified as "servants," not the bride, even in the final scene (compare with Matthew 25:14–30).

> "And there shall be no more curse, but the throne of God and of the Lamb shall be in it, and His servants shall serve Him. They shall see His face, and His name shall be on their foreheads." (Revelation 22:3–4)

iii) Non-Elect Salvation for Gentiles — identified as the "thirsty" who are invited to drink freely (compare with Matthew 25:31–46).

> "And the Spirit and the bride say, 'Come!' And let him who hears say, 'Come!' And let him who thirsts come. Whoever desires, let him take the water of life freely." (Revelation 22:17)

This interpretation maintains the integrity of the literal Chiliasm model while opening the possibility that non-elect individuals—both Israelites and Gentiles—may be granted salvation at the end of the Millennial Reign. The timeline and prophetic framework of Revelation, supported by insights from early Church Fathers, appear to affirm this structure.

WATER OF LIFE

The term "water of life" appears in several passages in the Book of Revelation, each situated within a specific prophetic timeline. The first reference occurs in **Revelation 7:9–17**, which takes place immediately after the First Resurrection. This scene depicts the saved multitude—Christians—receiving the water of life during Christ's Millennial Reign on the restored old earth.

> "...for the Lamb who is in the midst of the throne will shepherd them and lead them to living fountains of waters. And God will wipe away every tear from their eyes" (Revelation 7:17).

This is consistent with the image of the elect being raised in sinless human bodies and given access to the "fountain of life," administered through the direct reign of Christ. The location is still the present earth and heaven, albeit renewed and governed in righteousness.

The final mention of the "water of life" occurs in **Revelation 22:1–2 and 22:17**, which takes place after the Great White Throne Judgment and the creation of the new heavens and the new earth. The sequence of events is critical here, for by the time of Revelation 22, the results of the Book of Life have already been revealed (Revelation 20:11–15), and the final eternal states have begun. Here, the water of life flows from the throne of God into the New Jerusalem:

> "And he showed me a pure river of water of life, clear as crystal, proceeding from the throne of God and of the Lamb. In the middle of its street, and on either side of the river, was the tree of life..." (Revelation 22:1–2).

Then, in **Revelation 22:17**, the Spirit and the Bride extend an open invitation:

> "And the Spirit and the bride say, 'Come!' And let him who hears say, 'Come!' And let him who thirsts come. Whoever desires, let him take the water of life freely."

This last call does not appear to be directed toward the Bride herself, who has already partaken. Rather, it seems to be issued from the glorified Bride to others—those not previously part of the elect. This could represent the nations who are saved but not part of the Church, now offered the water of life freely. This call occurs post-judgment and post-consummation, suggesting that it applies to a distinct group who are not the glorified saints of the First Resurrection.

Some may argue that the "water of life" in both passages refers to the same salvation, but the textual evidence and prophetic context imply otherwise. In Revelation 7, it is Christ Himself who provides the water to His Church during the millennial age. In Revelation 22, it is the glorified Bride who joins the Spirit in extending the invitation to others. That implies a progression in redemptive history—from the redemption of the elect during the First Resurrection to the possibility of non-elect redemption at the final stage.

In the Chiliasm timeline, these are not concurrent events but two distinct moments of divine grace separated by 1,000 years. Christians receive the water of life first, at the beginning of Christ's reign. Then, after the judgment, the water of life flows into the renewed earth, and those among the saved nations are invited to partake of it as well.

This distinction is consistent with the nature of the final order. Revelation 21:24 speaks of "the nations of those who are saved" walking by the light of the New Jerusalem, while Revelation 21:27 emphasizes that "only those who are written in the Lamb's Book of Life" may enter the city itself. The water of life, in this sense, is offered outside the city as well—flowing from the throne but reaching even those not among the glorified elect.

Thus, the two references to the water of life are best understood as two separate stages of redemptive access. One is reserved for the elect during the Millennial Reign, and the other is granted to the saved nations after Judgment Day.

WATER OF LIFE BIBLE VERSES COMPARISON

A careful comparison of key verses concerning the "water of life" demonstrates a separation in both setting and recipients. While each reference refers to the same life-giving source—Christ—the context shows distinct applications across different eschatological stages in the Chiliasm framework.

Revelation 7:17 speaks of the Lamb shepherding the elect and leading them to the fountains of living water:

> "...for the Lamb who is in the midst of the throne will shepherd them and lead them to living fountains of waters. And God will wipe away every tear from their eyes."

This describes the First Resurrection—the Church triumphant. These saints have already attained immortality in a sinless human body and reign with Christ during the 1,000-year millennial kingdom. The setting here is still the restored old earth and heavens, as Revelation 20 has not yet occurred.

In contrast, **Revelation 22:1–2** portrays a different stage:

> "And he showed me a pure river of water of life, clear as crystal, proceeding from the throne of God and of the Lamb. In the middle of its street, and on either side of the river, was the tree of life..."

This is the final scene—after the creation of the new heavens and new earth, and after the Great White Throne Judgment. The water of life now flows within the New Jerusalem, and the tree of life is seen producing fruit for the healing of the nations. The elect have already been changed from human to "no more flesh and blood," that is, into celestial bodies. They no longer require this external administration of life because they are "one flesh" with Christ.

Then **Revelation 22:17** issues an open invitation:

> "And the Spirit and the bride say, 'Come!' And let him who hears say, 'Come!' And let him who thirsts come. Whoever desires, let him take the water of life freely."

This cannot refer to the Bride herself, since she is already glorified and fully united with Christ. Rather, this call appears to reach out to the "nations of those who are saved" (Revelation 21:24), who live outside the New Jerusalem in the renewed earth. These individuals may have been saved after the final judgment and granted non-elect salvation. They retain terrestrial resurrection bodies and require access to the water of life flowing from the throne to sustain their life.

So in summary:

At the start of the 1,000 years, the Church—resurrected in sinless human bodies—receives the water of life directly from Christ, in a restored but still corruptible creation. The Bride is nourished, comforted, and preserved.

At the end of the 1,000 years, following the final judgment, the water of life continues to flow—this time for the nations of the saved who were not part of the First Resurrection. These are invited to drink freely, not as members of the Bride, but as guests of the renewed kingdom, dwelling on the new earth and benefitting from the presence of God in the city they may approach, though not necessarily enter.

This progression reinforces the doctrine that the water of life is made available in two stages: first to the elect at the beginning of the Millennial Kingdom, and then to the non-elect saved after the Final Judgment.

THE THOUSAND YEARS

The phrase "thousand years" is not symbolic in the Chiliasm framework but refers to a literal 1,000-year reign of Christ on the present earth after His Second Coming. This period, also called the Millennial Reign, is mentioned six times in Revelation 20:1–7. There is no biblical basis for allegorizing this timeframe, especially since the rest of the passage is filled with literal sequences: Satan is bound, the saints reign, and the rest of the dead do not live again until the thousand years are finished.

During this period, Christians are raised in sinless, immortal human bodies (not yet celestial) to reign with Christ. Revelation 20:4–6 describes this resurrection and reign:

> "And they lived and reigned with Christ for a thousand years. But the rest of the dead did not live again until the thousand years were finished. This is the first resurrection. Blessed and holy is he who has part in the first resurrection. Over such the second death has no power, but they shall be priests of God and of Christ, and shall reign with Him a thousand years."

This reign takes place in the current heavens and earth, which have not yet fled away (Revelation 20:11). It is not the final state, as death, rebellion, and judgment still remain at the end of this period (Revelation 20:7–15). The Church—raised to rule—experiences the full measure of reward on this present creation, affirming Christ's words that the meek shall inherit the earth (Matthew 5:5).

Satan is released at the end of the 1,000 years to test the nations. This leads to the final rebellion, which is swiftly crushed. Then comes the Great White Throne Judgment, at which time the dead are judged, and the present heavens and earth are removed. Only then are the new heavens and the new earth introduced, along with the New Jerusalem descending from heaven (Revelation 21:1–2).

It is only after this entire process that the full transformation occurs: the Church is glorified in celestial bodies, the wicked are judged, and the "nations who are saved" appear—those who may represent the non-elect who are granted life on the final new earth. These events mark the boundary between the two water of life references previously examined.

Thus, the "thousand years" are not a vague metaphor for an unspecified church age, as some claim. Rather, it is a divinely appointed span of time between the First Resurrection and the General Resurrection, where the distinction between elect and non-elect becomes most visible.

Those in the First Resurrection reign as kings and priests and partake of the water of life during the Millennial Reign. Those in the General Resurrection, raised at the end of the thousand years, may be judged either unto condemnation or unto a form of salvation that is lesser in glory—yet genuine nonetheless. This division preserves the justice of God, the free will of man, and the graduated nature of resurrection glory as described in 1 Corinthians 15:38–42.

NON-ELECT SALVATION POSSIBILITY QUOTES

This is not a complete list but an instructional compilation, showcasing quotations from early Christians who affirmed Chiliasm and who may also imply two types of salvation—one for the elect and another possibly for the non-elect. When these quotes are aligned with the previously discussed thousand-year time gap, they provide a framework for placing the second resurrection to life at the end of that interval, distinct from the first resurrection. This separation is crucial. The later references to the "water of life" might then be seen as invitations offered to the non-elect, extending salvation to them after the millennium. These insights, paired with the church fathers' teachings cited here, suggest a consistent pattern in early Christian thought that supports this view.

Justin Martyr

i. Possible Non-Elect Salvation: The Wicked Becoming Submissive as One Child (Non-Elect)

In *Dialogue with Trypho*, Justin Martyr draws from Isaiah 53 and interprets the prophetic language in a way that hints at the eventual obedience of the wicked:

> "We have preached before Him as if [He were] a child, as if a root in a dry ground." (And what follows in order of the prophecy already quoted.) But when the passage speaks as from the lips of many, 'We have preached before Him,' and adds, 'as if a child,' it signifies that the wicked shall become subject to Him, and shall

obey His command, and that all shall become as one child … and of those things which would also be done by Christ Himself.

This interpretation presents the wicked not merely as condemned but as those who may come under Christ's authority and become obedient. The phrase "as one child" suggests an image of submissiveness and potential restoration, though distinct from the intimate union of the elect.

ii. Elect Salvation: The Church as an Analogy

Justin then makes a contrast by describing the elect as the body of Christ—unified and predetermined in belief:

> "Such a thing [analogy] as you may witness in the body [Christians]: although the members are enumerated as many, all are called one, and are a body. For, indeed, a commonwealth and a church, though many individuals in number, are in fact as one, called and addressed by one appellation … of those who it was foreknown were to believe in Him."

This elect group is united in faith and foreknown in belief. The key difference is that they are not described as becoming subject, but rather as already belonging to Christ, with their union compared to a living body. Thus, while the wicked are described as being made subject (non-elect salvation), the church is already one with Christ (elect salvation).

Irenaeus of Lyons

Irenaeus distinguishes between those who receive inheritance now and others who are let go or saved only at the time of the final judgment—presumably after the Millennium. This sequence is important. Those who miss the "wedding" of the Lamb—described elsewhere as the first resurrection—are not necessarily doomed. Instead, they may still be saved at the general judgment, possibly corresponding to the non-elect.

He writes:

> "When God takes vengeance, in the one case indeed typically, temporarily, and more moderately … For those points to which they call attention with regard to the God who then awarded temporal punishments to the unbelieving … these same [facts, I say,] shall nevertheless repeat themselves in the Lord, who judges for eternity those whom He does judge, and lets go free for eternity those whom He does let go free."

Here, the two groups—those eternally judged and those eternally freed—are addressed in the context of the final judgment, not the millennial reign. This strongly implies that the group let go for eternity is different from the elect who reign with Christ in the millennium.

He continues:

> "And again, who are they that have been saved and received the inheritance? Those, doubtless, who do believe God, and who have continued in His love; as did Caleb [the son] of Jephunneh and Joshua [the son] of Nun (Numbers 14:30), and innocent children, who have had no sense of evil. But who are they that are saved now…"

This passage clarifies that the elect—those saved now and inheriting the kingdom—are the believers who live righteously in this life. Those judged afterward—at the second resurrection—are therefore a distinct group. Their potential salvation does not make them elect, but it does make them recipients of divine mercy.

Papias of Hierapolis

Though the writings of Papias survive only in quotations from later authors, his chiliastic position is uncontested. He clearly believed in a literal thousand-year reign of Christ on earth, following the resurrection of the righteous.

He is recorded as saying:

> "There will be a period of a thousand years after the resurrection of the dead, when the kingdom of Christ will be set up on this earth in a material form."

This implies that the resurrection he refers to is the first resurrection—the resurrection of the righteous. By necessity, the rest of the dead are raised only after this period ends, as Revelation 20:5 teaches: "The rest of the dead did not come to life until the thousand years were ended." Papias, then, makes room for two distinct resurrections. Those who arise later could include non-elect souls who receive life at the end of the millennium.

Tertullian

In *Against Marcion*, Tertullian affirms a literal thousand-year kingdom and associates it with the reward of the faithful. But significantly, he also alludes to further judgment and restoration after the millennial reign. He writes:

> "We do confess that a kingdom is promised to us upon the earth, although before heaven, only in another state of existence; inasmuch as it will be after the resurrection for a thousand years in the divinely-built city of Jerusalem."

This statement reflects the same chiliastic structure: the elect are raised to inherit the kingdom in the thousand-year reign, while other events—including final judgment and possibly the restoration of others—happen afterward. Though Tertullian does not elaborate on non-elect salvation, the possibility remains in the structure he affirms.

These early chiliasts—Justin, Irenaeus, Papias, and Tertullian—recognized two crucial realities: a millennial reign following the resurrection of the elect, and a final judgment or release that takes place afterward. Their writings suggest that those who are not included in the first resurrection are not necessarily condemned. Instead, there may yet be hope for their redemption at the second resurrection. This possibility aligns with Revelation's offer that "whosoever will" may freely take of the water of life (Revelation 22:17). Such an invitation, coming after the Millennium in the biblical narrative, suggests a genuine opportunity for salvation extended even to those outside the elect. Thus, early Christianity may have held to a theology broad enough to include non-elect salvation without compromising the distinct inheritance of the elect.

POST MORTEM SALVATION

Tertullian believed in a form of purgatorial experience in Hades, particularly in connection with Christ's statements about judgment "until the last penny" (Matthew 5:26). He interpreted these verses as describing a postmortem judgment involving punishment that ends only when the full penalty is paid. This interpretation naturally lends itself to a view that includes the possibility of postmortem salvation.

Irenaeus also references these same verses, though he does not explicitly state whether salvation is possible after such spirit-world judgment. His silence on the matter neither affirms nor denies the possibility but leaves room for interpretation.

Justin Martyr presents a noteworthy possibility for non-elect salvation. He describes certain individuals as so wicked that they were unable to ascend from the punitive regions of the spirit world. However, he simultaneously implies that some may have successfully ascended out of these regions after enduring their punishment. He writes, "unless they had paid the full penalty," suggesting that, for some, the punishment is not eternal but terminable. This choice of words implies the existence of a class of condemned individuals who are later released—potentially pointing to a form of salvation after judgment in the afterlife.

Christ Himself describes this same "judgment until the last penny" in a context involving "torturers" (Matthew 18:34), further strengthening the interpretation that this pertains to postmortem judgment. It is also significant that this punishment is not exclusive to the righteous but is aimed at the wicked. If Tertullian is correct in believing that those who endure this judgment are eventually saved, then the implications are profound: even the "wicked servant" may be saved after undergoing divine judgment.

Consider Christ's words in Matthew 18:32–35:

> "Then his master, after he had called him, said to him, 'You wicked servant! I forgave you all that debt because you begged me. Should you not also have had compassion on your fellow servant, just as I had pity on you?'
>
> And his master was angry, and delivered him to the torturers until he should pay all that was due to him.
>
> So My heavenly Father also will do to you if each of you, from his heart, does not forgive his brother his trespasses."

This passage clearly distinguishes between the mercy initially granted and the subsequent punishment imposed. If, as Tertullian understood it, the "wicked servant" ultimately pays his debt through torment and is then released, such a restoration could qualify as a form of non-elect salvation.

Importantly, it is difficult to imagine Christ including such a person in His bride, which is consistently portrayed as consisting only of those with sincere repentance and good works accomplished during their earthly lives. Those saved only after judgment, in this context, would not be part of the elect. They are not the overcomers who inherit the kingdom, but rather recipients of mercy after the fact. This crucial distinction upholds the concept of non-elect salvation without compromising the integrity of the elect's special inheritance.

Additionally, Matthew 18 describes this man as a "wicked servant," a designation that appears incompatible with the Roman Catholic view that this passage refers to "faithful Catholics with lighter sins." Christ's use of the term "wicked" is strong. It aligns this individual more closely with the unbeliever than with the penitent faithful. Luke 12:46 corroborates this when Christ declares that the master will "cut him in pieces and assign him a place with the unbelievers." This comparison strengthens the argument that Christ views such a servant in the same category as unbelievers. Consequently, if Tertullian's interpretation holds—that such a person could still be saved post-judgment—then it opens the door for some unbelievers to be saved after their spirit-world punishment, if God wills it.

Irenaeus also provides support for this view in a passage where he uses the language of Christ descending "to the things of the earth beneath" to seek the sheep that had perished. This imagery, drawn from the parable of the lost sheep, is applied here to the context of the afterlife. Irenaeus connects Christ's descent to the spirit world with the act of seeking and saving the lost, even those who are not currently part of the elect. He writes that Christ:

> "descend[ed] to those things which are of the earth beneath, seeking the sheep which had perished,"

He further links this salvation to the fulfillment of a temporal condemnation, suggesting that these individuals are saved only after a certain punishment has been satisfied. He writes of:

> "remaining part of the body—[namely, the body] of everyman who is found in life—when the time is fulfilled of that condemnation which existed by reason of disobedience, [they] may arise,"

This implies that some may join the resurrection of life only after completing their assigned period of judgment. They are not among the elect who are raised at the first resurrection but are instead resurrected at the second, having been purified in the spirit world. Such individuals, while not inheriting the kingdom as kings and priests, may still receive life—eternal life—albeit in a different and subordinate capacity.

Therefore, both Irenaeus and Tertullian allow for the possibility that certain wicked persons may be saved after judgment in the afterlife, not because of works done in this life, but because of a divine mercy extended after they have borne the due penalty for their disobedience. Justin Martyr, though more implicit in his comments, seems to allow for a similar idea in his recognition that some are unable to ascend unless they have "paid the full penalty."

This view of postmortem salvation does not erase the doctrine of eternal condemnation. Rather, it limits eternal destruction to those who remain impenitent. It distinguishes between the elect—those raised at the first resurrection to inherit the kingdom—and those who are not elect but are nonetheless recipients of divine mercy after postmortem correction. The difference is not in whether both are saved, but in when and how they are saved, and what reward they inherit.

Thus, a consistent reading of these early church fathers—combined with Christ's own teachings—suggests that salvation after death may be possible for some. However, such individuals would not be counted among the elect. They are not the bride. They do not rule with Christ. Their salvation is real, but their place is different, and their restoration occurs only after judgment has run its course.

CONCLUSION

What if non-elect salvation turns out to be false?

Through the prophet Jeremiah, God warned that if a man delivers a prophecy or oracle as his own attempt, even if it turns out to be incorrect, he bears no eternal guilt—because he did not falsely invoke the name of Jehovah. However, if someone claims "God told me so," when in fact He did not, or if the prophecy fails to come to pass, that person incurs everlasting shame or judgment. The seriousness of this error is underscored by the Hebrew word *olam*, which appears twice in that context and is translated as "everlasting" and "perpetual" (Jeremiah 23:36–40). This distinction makes it clear: declaring speculative interpretations as personal reasoning—even if mistaken—does not carry the same consequence as falsely speaking in God's name.

What if non-elect salvation turns out to be true?

If the possibility of non-elect salvation is ultimately validated, then the "few" who are saved (as Christ described) would refer specifically to the elect—those who become His Bride and inherit the heavenly Jerusalem. These elect saints are raised in the first resurrection and dwell in heaven forever (Revelation 20:4–6; Revelation 21:2–3).

In contrast, Christ's ransom "for many" (Mark 10:45; Matthew 20:28) could include not only the elect but also a broader category—those saved as non-elect. These would inherit not the heavens, but the final new earth. Revelation 22:17 shows the Bride, already glorified, calling others to come and "take the water of life freely." This language implies that others—those outside the Bride—are still being offered salvation at this stage. The source of that water is Christ, and it flows into the final new earth (Revelation 22:1–

2). Those who dwell there are also granted healing from the leaves of the tree of life.

This healing is significant. It likely refers to those who are not part of the glorified Bride, but rather the saved nations—people who may have been "saved by fire" as described in 1 Corinthians 3:15. Since Christians, under the Chiliasm model, are already raised and perfected 1,000 years earlier, it would not make theological sense for them to require such healing in this final scene. Instead, these healed ones could be the non-elect who are granted mercy on the final new earth.

This might be the meaning behind the words of the prophet Daniel: "Many shall be purified" (Daniel 12:10). That could be referring to those who are "saved by fire," not as part of the elect, but as a separate group. If this is correct, then non-elect salvation offers a biblical explanation for verses that suggest a greater number being saved than those identified strictly as believers. In such a case, believers would represent a subset of the larger number of redeemed.

The theological concept of non-elect salvation is relatively new and still emerging through ongoing scholarly exploration. It is not a formal doctrine, nor can it be confirmed with certainty at this time. Therefore, any such interpretation must be approached cautiously—as a speculative academic hypothesis rather than a dogmatic assertion. The goal in presenting it is to demonstrate that this reading matches a literal and coherent interpretation of Scripture and is thus a valid possibility for consideration.

A responsible discussion of prophecy should never rely solely on private opinion. That is why this exploration has drawn heavily from the writings of renowned early Church Fathers who affirmed Chiliasm. By grounding the argument in their testimony, this study avoids becoming a subjective theory. Even if this interpretation later proves incorrect, God sees the honesty of the effort. The evidence cited was real, the method faithful, and the claim never presented as direct revelation from God. In such cases, it is reasonable to believe that God, in His righteousness, would not condemn an honest inquiry made with reverence and humility.

CHAPTER 4 Shadow of Death: A Prophetic Glimpse into Spirit World Salvation

INTRODUCTION

The Hebrew word וְצַלְמָוֶת (*wə·ṣal·mā·weṯ*), commonly translated as *"shadow of death"*—and referred to throughout this essay simply as "the phrase"—may indicate regions within the spirit world associated with judgment in Hell. If that is the case, then the key passage in **Psalm 107:10–15** could potentially describe a form of non-elect salvation granted to **some** who are delivered after enduring judgment in Hell.

In modern English usage, the phrase *"shadow of death"* typically refers to people who are alive but facing imminent death, such as in cases of severe illness or trauma. However, in biblical contexts, especially within Hebrew linguistics, the term can carry broader theological connotations. It can represent a state of spiritual death or separation from God due to sin. It may also symbolically describe a period of mourning or affliction, such as grief after the loss of a loved one.

SHADOW OF DEATH IN THE BIBLE

God's direct usage of the mysterious Hebrew term וְצַלְמָוֶת (*wə·ṣal·mā·weṯ*), translated as *"shadow of death"*, appears prominently in His discourse with Job. This is significant, as the context strongly implies the spirit world, especially since the word *death* appears alongside the imagery of "gates." The reference to "gates of death" may suggest access into and out of punitive regions, and the accompanying term *shadow* can imply an intermediate state. God asks:

> "Have the gates of death been revealed to you? Or have you seen the doors of the shadow of death?" (Job 38:17)

Such terminology suggests more than poetic language. It likely alludes to a structured spiritual reality involving places of judgment or punishment beyond physical death.

A particularly striking passage that may describe a case of non-elect salvation is **Psalm 107:10–15**, where the phrase *shadow of death* appears again. The text plainly states that these individuals *rebelled* against God and *rejected* His will—yet they were eventually saved after enduring judgment. It reads:

"There were those who lived in darkness and in the shadow of
death,
Prisoners in misery and chains,
Because they had rebelled against the words of God
And rejected the plan of the Most High.
Therefore He humbled their heart with labor;
They stumbled and there was no one to help.
Then they cried out to the LORD in their trouble;
He saved them from their distresses.
He brought them out of darkness and the shadow of death
And broke their bands apart.
They shall give thanks to the LORD for His mercy,
And for His wonders to the sons of mankind!
For He has shattered gates of bronze
And cut off bars of iron." (Psalm 107:10–16)

The Septuagint preserves the same essential meaning:

"Even them that sit in darkness and the shadow of death,
Fettered in poverty and iron;
Because they rebelled against the words of God,
And provoked the counsel of the Most High.
So their heart was brought low with troubles;
They were weak, and there was no helper.
Then they cried to the Lord in their affliction,
And He saved them out of their distresses.
And He brought them out of darkness and the shadow of death,
And broke their bonds asunder.
Let them acknowledge to the Lord His mercies,
And His wonders to the children of men.
For He broke to pieces the brazen gates,
And crushed the iron bars." (Psalm 106:10–16 LXX)

This passage strongly suggests the recipients of this deliverance were not among the faithful. They had *rebelled* and *rejected* God's counsel—yet were delivered after crying out. That this took place in the *shadow of death* implies a spirit-world judgment context. Several other passages support this reading.

I. Job 3:3–5 – Shadow of Death as Spirit World Darkness

Job laments the day of his birth, wishing it had perished in darkness. The phrase *shadow of death* here appears to describe a realm opposite to the day of birth—namely, the realm of death:

"May the day perish on which I was born,
And the night in which it was said, 'A male child is conceived.' …
May darkness and the shadow of death claim it;
May a cloud settle on it;
May the blackness of the day terrify it." (Job 3:3,5)

This passage, often studied for its depth of psychological anguish, may also suggest a theological interpretation of death as an actual spiritual region—something Job clearly dreads yet contemplates deeply.

II. Job 10:19–22 – The Shadow of Death as the Place One Does Not Return From

Here Job explicitly refers to the journey after death as going to the land of darkness and the *shadow of death*. His description emphasizes its finality:

"I would have been as though I had not been.
I would have been carried from the womb to the grave.
Are not my days few? Cease! Leave me alone, that I may take a
little comfort,
Before I go to the place from which I shall not return,
To the land of darkness and the shadow of death,
A land as dark as darkness itself,
As the shadow of death, without any order,
Where even the light is like darkness." (Job 10:19–22)

This passage reveals Job's understanding that the *shadow of death* is not metaphorical but refers to a literal domain beyond life—one that is disorderly, bleak, and permanent for those who enter.

III. Job 28:3 – The Depths of the Earth as Shadow of Death

Here, the phrase is used to describe the physical depths searched by man for minerals. Yet the language evokes parallels to the underworld or the hidden spirit world:

> "Man puts an end to darkness,
> And searches every recess
> For ore in the darkness and the shadow of death." (Job 28:3)

Since the spirit world is commonly associated with the lower regions of the earth, this verse offers a figurative bridge between earthly and spiritual depths. It mirrors the belief that the shadow of death is tied to a subterranean realm where souls await judgment.

Modern science has also speculated about parallel dimensions. If the spirit world exists as a layer below or beyond our own, as these verses suggest, it would remain undetectable until empirical instruments are capable of interfacing with that realm. Until then, it is a matter of faith—the evidence of things not seen (Hebrews 11:1).

IV. Psalm 44:19 – Shadow of Death and Dragons

In this verse, the phrase is paired with "dragons," likely symbolizing spiritual forces or desolate realms:

> "Though thou hast sore broken us in the place of dragons,
> And covered us with the shadow of death." (Psalm 44:19, KJV)

The Hebrew root supports the translation of *dragons*, though some scholars argue it may refer to *jackals*. The Septuagint omits either term and simply reads:

> "For thou hast laid us low in a place of affliction,
> And the shadow of death has covered us." (Psalm 43:19 LXX)

Regardless of translation differences, this passage evokes a vivid image of suffering in a forsaken place. Many commentators interpret it allegorically, but that need not exclude a literal spirit-world application.

V. Psalm 107:10–12 – Spirit World Judgment in the Shadow of Death

As previously discussed, this passage portrays those in the *shadow of death* not as righteous sufferers but as rebels who rejected God's Word. Their condition is described with terms such as *darkness, affliction, chains*, and *no helper*—all suggestive of punishment.

> "Those who sat in darkness and in the shadow of death,
> Bound in affliction and irons—

Because they rebelled against the words of God,
And despised the counsel of the Most High,
Therefore He brought down their heart with labor;
They fell down, and there was none to help." (Psalm 107:10–12)

These are not saints, but sinners. Their redemption is not from temporary hardship but from divine punishment.

VI. Psalm 107:13–15 – Divine Mercy and Possible Non-Elect Salvation

What follows confirms the theme of deliverance. Despite their rebellion, they are saved—possibly representing a class of non-elect who receive mercy after judgment:

"Then they cried out to the Lord in their trouble,
And He saved them out of their distresses.
He brought them out of darkness and the shadow of death,
And broke their chains in pieces.
Oh, that men would give thanks to the Lord for His goodness,
And for His wonderful works to the children of men!" (Psalm 107:13–15)

This could point to a real example of non-elect salvation, where mercy is granted after a period of affliction in a spirit-world judgment context.

Some scholars argue that Psalm 107 refers primarily to Israel's historical bondage in Egypt or Babylon and apply these verses allegorically. However, such historical applications do not invalidate a literal interpretation as well. Dual fulfillment or layered meanings are a well-established principle in biblical prophecy and typology—especially when other texts and contexts support it.

VII. Jeremiah 2:6 – A Contested Usage

This final occurrence is used by some to claim all shadow of death references point only to earthly suffering, such as Israel's exodus or Babylonian captivity:

"Neither did they say, 'Where is the LORD,
Who brought us up out of the land of Egypt,
Who led us through the wilderness,
Through a land of deserts and pits,

Through a land of drought and the shadow of death,
Through a land that no one crossed
And where no one dwelt?"' (Jeremiah 2:6)

While this may point to a physical landscape, the language still describes a transitional or intermediate zone—one where no man crosses or dwells. This reinforces the connection to the spirit world as a desolate realm of separation, whether literal or symbolic.

Even if Jeremiah 2:6 refers only to earthly geography, it does not negate the more clearly spiritual usage of *shadow of death* in Job and Psalms. Thus, the overall biblical pattern strongly supports a reading in which *shadow of death* refers not just to hardship in life, but to the possibility of divine mercy after punishment in the afterlife—a plausible context for non-elect salvation.

SHADOW OF DEATH IN THE GOSPEL OF NICODEMUS

This section presents quotes from early Christian writings that support the idea that the phrase *"shadow of death"* refers to the spirit world, particularly its judgment regions. If this interpretation is accurate, then Psalm 107:10–15 could describe a form of non-elect salvation—for *some*, not all—after judgment, if God wills it. Thus, to argue this as a plausible biblical possibility (not a doctrine), it is necessary to demonstrate that *"shadow of death"* can indeed refer to the spiritual realm.

Although neither Justin of Rome nor Tertullian provide a direct use of the phrase *"shadow of death"* in this exact context (possibly due to loss of relevant portions of their writings), early sources such as Eusebius and others note that both men referenced a text known as the **Acts of Pilate** or **Acta Pilati**. This writing, though non-canonical, has been regarded by some Roman Catholic scholars as *orthodox and free of Gnostic taint*. It is also known under the name **Gospel of Nicodemus**, and within it we find a strong connection between the phrase *"shadow of death"* and the context of judgment in the spirit world—especially in reference to Psalm 107:10–16 and Matthew 4:15–16.

The following excerpt illustrates this clearly:

"The land of Zabulon and the land of Nephthalim across Jordan, Galilee of the nations, the people who sat in darkness, have seen a great light; and light was shining among those who are in the region of the shadow of death. And now it has come and shone upon us sitting in death."

And when all the saints heard this from Esaias, they said to Hades: *Open your gates. Since you are now conquered, you will be weak and powerless.*

And there was a great voice, as of thunders, saying: *Lift up your gates, you princes; and be lifted up, you infernal gates; and the King of glory shall come in.*

Hades, seeing that they had twice shouted out this, says, as if not knowing: *Who is the king of glory?*

David says, in answer to Hades: *I recognise those words of the shout, since I prophesied the same by His Spirit. And now, what I have said above I say to you, The Lord strong and mighty, the Lord mighty in battle; He is the King of glory.*

And the Lord Himself has looked down from heaven upon earth, to hear the groans of the prisoners, and to release the sons of the slain.

And now, most filthy and most foul Hades, open your gates, that the King of glory may come in.

While David was thus speaking, there came to Hades, in the form of a man, the Lord of majesty, and lighted up the eternal darkness, and burst asunder the indissoluble chains; and the aid of unconquered power visited *us*, sitting in the profound darkness of transgressions, and in the shadow of death of sins.

This passage is key. While it clearly refers to Christ's descent into Hades to rescue the saints (elect salvation), it also depicts *others*—those in *groaning, chains, sins, and transgressions* in the more "filthy" regions of Hades—as being freed as well. These may represent those outside the Bride of Christ. If so, it suggests a possible example of non-elect salvation.

Christ's own teaching in Luke 16:19–31, which describes Hades as divided between comfort and torment, corresponds to this portrayal. The Gospel of Nicodemus, while not Scripture, aligns with Jewish thought and early Christian tradition about compartmentalization in the spirit world.

All known variants of the Gospel of Nicodemus, particularly Part II, preserve this possible non-elect salvation theme. For example, in the **Greek form of Part II**, the release of all the dead from the dark regions of Hades is described alongside the saints:

"Hades answered: … For, lo, all those that I have swallowed from eternity I perceive to be in commotion, and I am pained in my belly. And the snatching away of Lazarus beforehand seems to me to be no good sign: for not like a dead body, but like an eagle, he flew out of me; for so suddenly did the earth throw him out.

Wherefore also I adjure even you, for your benefit and for mine, not to bring him here; for I think that he is coming here to raise all the dead.

And this I tell you: by the darkness in which we live, if you bring him here, not one of the dead will be left behind in it to me.

… There came, then, again a voice saying: *Lift up the gates.*

Hades, hearing the voice the second time, answered as if not knowing, and says: *Who is this King of glory?*

The angels of the Lord say: *The Lord strong and mighty, the Lord mighty in battle.*

And immediately with these words the brazen gates were shattered, and the iron bars broken, and *all the dead who had been bound came out of the prisons*, and we with them.

And the King of glory came in in the form of a man, and *all the dark places of Hades were lighted up.*"

Here again, we see not just the saints being delivered, but *all the dead who had been bound*—a possible indication of salvation extended even to the unrighteous after judgment. If this is valid, it could support the notion of non-elect salvation.

The **second Latin form of Part II** continues the theme, using the exact phrase *shadow of death* to describe the lower world:

"I, Karinus. O Lord Jesus Christ, Son of the living God, permit me to speak of Your wonders which You have done in the lower world.

When, therefore, we were kept in darkness and the shadow of death in the lower world, suddenly there shone upon us a great light, and Hades and the gates of death trembled.

And then was heard the voice of the Son of the Father most high, as if the voice of a great thunder; and loudly proclaiming, He thus charged them: *Lift up your gates, you princes; lift up the everlasting gates; the King of glory, Christ the Lord, will come up to enter in.*

Then Satan, the leader of death, came up, fleeing in terror, saying to his officers and the powers below: *My officers, and all the powers below, run together, shut your gates, put up the iron bars, and fight bravely, and resist, lest they lay hold of us, and keep us captive in chains.*

Then all his impious officers were perplexed …

Then all the saints, hearing this again, exulted in joy.

And one of those standing round, Isaias by name, cried out aloud, and thundered: *Father Adam, and all standing round, hear my declaration. When I was on earth, and by the teaching of the Holy Spirit, in prophecy I sang of this light: The people who sat in darkness have seen a great light; to them dwelling in the region of the shadow of death light has arisen.*

… Then the Saviour, inquiring thoroughly about all, seized Hades, immediately threw some down into Tartarus, and led *some* with Him to the upper world."

This final statement reinforces the key point: *not all* in Hades were saved. The Lord separated individuals—throwing some into Tartarus (reserved for final punishment) and leading others to the upper world. Among those who were saved were some who had been *kept in chains*, called "us" in the account. These could represent non-elect individuals who were granted mercy following judgment.

Regardless of whether this passage applies exclusively to people in the past, it aligns well with the interpretation of Psalm 107:10–16, which describes individuals saved *after* being judged in Hades-like conditions. If these persons are not the Bride of Christ—who must be made up of the faithful, the righteous, and those who lived in obedience—then they may represent a distinct group: those who are saved, but not glorified.

Such a group may correspond to those who inherit the **final new earth** as *nations of the saved* (Revelation 21:24–26), distinguished from the Bride who inherits the New Jerusalem. All Christians are called *priests* and *kings* (Revelation 1:6; 1 Peter 2:9), and the Church Fathers consistently affirm this. Thus, if any are saved but do not share this priestly status, they may belong to a non-elect category—redeemed by God's mercy but not glorified in the heavenly realm.

SHADOW OF DEATH IN CHURCH FATHERS

To strengthen the possibility that the phrase *"shadow of death"* refers to the spirit world—including both judgment and comfort regions—it is important to examine how early church fathers used the expression. These historical witnesses do not always comment directly on the punishment aspects of Hades, yet their writings consistently confirm that *"shadow of death"* was understood as referring to the intermediate realm where souls await resurrection, which supports the interpretation of Psalm 107:10–16 as potentially describing non-elect salvation.

Irenaeus of Lyons (c. 130–202 C.E.) offers a clear example. In his defense of the bodily resurrection, he rebukes those who spiritualize Ephesians 4:9–10 and deny the intermediate state. He affirms that Christ descended *bodily* into the regions of the dead—*"the shadow of death"*—and will raise His disciples likewise:

> "[If all these things occurred, I say], how must these men not be put to confusion, who allege that the lower parts refer to this world of ours, but that their inner man, leaving the body here, ascends into the super-celestial place? For as the Lord went away in the midst of the shadow of death, where the souls of the dead were, yet afterwards arose in the body, and after the resurrection was taken up [into heaven], it is manifest that the souls of His disciples also, upon whose account the Lord underwent these things, shall go away into the invisible place allotted to them by God, and there remain until the resurrection, awaiting that event; then receiving their bodies, and rising in their entirety, that is bodily, just as the Lord arose, they shall come thus into the presence of God."

Irenaeus plainly connects *"the shadow of death"* to the unseen realm, the intermediate state for disembodied souls. While he does not dwell on the torment regions, he affirms that souls of Christ's disciples remain in the invisible place until the resurrection. This directly affirms the theological ground on which the possibility of non-elect salvation rests.

An anonymous patristic homily often titled **"Ancient Homily for Holy Saturday"** likewise refers to *"shadow of death"* unmistakably in the context of the spirit world. Some scholars attribute this homily to **Melito of Sardis** (c. 100–180 C.E.), though authorship is uncertain:

> "Something strange is happening — there is a great silence on earth today, a great silence and stillness. The whole earth keeps

silence because the King is asleep. The earth trembled and is still because God has fallen asleep in the flesh and he has raised up all who have slept ever since the world began. God has died in the flesh and hell trembles with fear.

He has gone to search for our first parent, as for a lost sheep. Greatly desiring to visit those who live in darkness and in the shadow of death, he has gone to free from sorrow the captives Adam and Eve, he who is both God and the son of Eve."

This homily explicitly equates *"shadow of death"* with the spiritual condition of those in Hades. Adam and Eve are referred to as captives in sorrow, yet are among those delivered. The reference to freeing the captives from this darkness reflects both the hope of elect salvation and the possibility of other souls—such as the patriarchs or those righteous-by-conscience—being liberated from death's dominion.

Gregory Thaumaturgus (c. 213–270 C.E.), a bishop known for his miraculous ministry and theological clarity, also uses the phrase *"shadow of death"* to describe the spirit world. In a homily celebrating the Virgin Mary, he draws upon the image of Christ as the illumining pearl who enters the darkness to rescue souls:

> "Let us twine, as with a wreath, the souls [of them that love the festival and love to hearken] with golden blossoms, fain to be crowned with wreaths from the unfading gardens; and offering in our hands the fair-fruited flowers of Christ, let us gather [them]. For the God-like temple of the Holy Virgin is meet to be glorified with such a crown; because the illumining Pearl cometh forth, to the end that it may raise up again into the ever-streaming light *them that were gone down into darkness and the shadow of death.*"

Here, the phrase *"gone down into… the shadow of death"* clearly describes those who have entered the spirit world. Christ's mission is described as bringing them into eternal light, again alluding to a post-mortem rescue that may include those beyond the elect.

Melito of Sardis also provides a distinct use of *"shadow of death"* in his renowned work *On the Passover*. In his rich typological reflection, he describes humanity's condition under death's dominion before Christ:

> "Humanity was doled out by death, for a strange disaster and captivity surrounded him; he was dragged off a captive under the shadow of death, and the father's image was left desolate. For this reason in the body of the Lord is the paschal mystery completed."

This statement does not simply refer to physical death but to a spiritual captivity—*"under the shadow of death"*—that Christ broke through in His Passion. This supports the notion that the phrase can carry the meaning of spiritual bondage in the afterlife.

Finally, **John of Damascus** (c. 675–749 C.E.), often considered the last of the Greek Church Fathers, clearly uses *"shadow of death"* in reference to punishment regions in Hades. In his theological reflection, he affirms that Christ brought light into this realm, offering salvation to those who believed after seeing Him—even among the bound:

> "The soul when it was deified descended into Hades, in order that, just as the Sun of Righteousness rose for those upon the earth, so likewise He might bring light to those who sit under the earth in darkness and shadow of death: in order that just as He brought the message of peace to those upon the earth, and of release to the prisoners, and of sight to the blind, and became to those who believed the Author of everlasting salvation and to those who did not believe a reproach of their unbelief, so He might become the same to those in Hades: That every knee should bow to Him, of things in heaven, and things in earth and things under the earth. And thus after He had freed those who had been bound for ages, straightway He rose again from the dead, shewing us the way of resurrection."

John's words powerfully affirm the reach of Christ's descent. Not only does he refer to the *"shadow of death"* as a literal place within Hades, but he also notes that some who had been bound for ages were **freed**. Others remained condemned, reproached for unbelief—even in that realm. This shows that some believed **after seeing Christ**, a situation that may reflect the non-elect salvation possibility. Such individuals are clearly not the Bride of Christ or His priestly people (Revelation 1:6), but they may yet receive mercy.

These patristic writings support the understanding that the *"shadow of death"* is more than poetic language—it often refers to a real region of the intermediate state. Whether in comforting or punishing compartments, it is repeatedly linked with Christ's descent into Hades, His proclamation of victory, and in some cases, the release of prisoners. If Psalm 107:10–16 refers to a class of such souls—those who rebelled but later cried out and were rescued—then non-elect salvation remains a viable theological possibility grounded in both Scripture and early Christian testimony.

SHADOW OF DEATH IN MODERN USAGE

Even in contemporary literature, the phrase *"shadow of death"* is used in ways that align with its traditional association with the spirit world. One noteworthy modern example appears in the writings of **C. S. Lewis**, author of *The Chronicles of Narnia*. Though not a theologian in the systematic sense, Lewis reflects theological concepts that intersect with the idea of non-elect salvation. In *The Great Divorce*, Lewis portrays a fictional narrative of souls traveling between a "grey town" and a heavenly realm, guided by spiritual insight.

The following exchange in the book uses the term *"Valley of the Shadow of Death"* to distinguish those who remain in rebellion from those who journey toward light:

> "I don't understand. Is judgment not final? Is there really a way out of Hell into Heaven?" MacDonald answers: "It depends on the way ye're using the words. If they leave that grey town behind it will not have been Hell. To any that leaves it, it is Purgatory. And perhaps ye had better not call this country Heaven. Not Deep Heaven, ye understand." (Here he smiled at me.) "Ye can call it the Valley of the Shadow of Life. And yet to those who stay here it will have been Heaven from the first. And ye can call those sad streets in the town yonder the Valley of the Shadow of Death: but to those who remain there they will have been Hell even from the beginning."

Here, Lewis uses the *"Valley of the Shadow of Death"* metaphorically, but not without theological weight. It is a realm of spiritual consequence—Hell for the unrepentant, and something else entirely for those who turn back toward light. This supports, at least narratively, the concept of **post-mortem transformation**, a critical component of the non-elect salvation possibility.

Lewis did not relegate such views to fiction alone. In a letter, he wrote of his personal belief in purgatory, despite his Protestant identity:

> "Of course I pray for the dead. … At our age the majority of those we love best are dead. … I believe in Purgatory. Mind you, the Reformers had good reasons for throwing doubt on 'the Romish doctrine concerning Purgatory' as that Romish doctrine had then become."

While his purgatorial belief does not align completely with the doctrine of non-elect salvation explored here, it illustrates that even respected modern

Christian thinkers have accepted **intermediate states** and **post-mortem purification**, ideas that overlap with this possibility.

CONCLUSION

Even if the literal phrase *"shadow of death"* in some contexts refers to earthly affliction or temporal suffering, many Scriptures demonstrate that it can simultaneously carry a **spirit-world meaning**. This twofold interpretation—where a single passage conveys both a literal and a deeper spiritual truth—is not uncommon in Scripture.

For instance, consider **Hosea 11:1**:

> "When Israel was a child, I loved him, And out of Egypt I called My son."

This clearly refers to the **historical exodus of Israel**. Yet in **Matthew 2:14–15**, the Gospel writer gives it a **Christological fulfillment**:

> "When he arose, he took the young Child and His mother by night and departed for Egypt, and was there until the death of Herod, that it might be fulfilled which was spoken by the Lord through the prophet, saying, 'Out of Egypt I called My Son.'"

Both meanings—literal and prophetic—are valid. In the same way, *"shadow of death"* may be used in Scripture to describe both a time of earthly peril and a **location or condition in the spirit world**. The same phrase can have layers of truth without contradiction.

Nevertheless, a **word of caution** is appropriate: Scripture must never be allegorized arbitrarily. Any suggestion of a dual meaning must be weighed carefully, and never promoted as doctrine unless it can be clearly established from the Word itself. Therefore, this interpretation of *"shadow of death"* as referring to the spirit world and to non-elect salvation must remain a **theological possibility**, not a demand of doctrine.

However, if this possibility is correct, then several difficult passages in Scripture take on clearer meaning. For example, the phrase *"saved, yet so as through fire"* (1 Corinthians 3:15) could describe one who is **delivered posthumously without reward**, possibly through a *believing-after-seeing* scenario implied in **John 6:29, 35–36, 40**.

In contrast, Christians—the elect—receive the *reward of the inheritance* (Colossians 3:24) and are symbolized as the *good ground* in the Parable of the Sower (Luke 8:15). Their salvation is not just a deliverance, but a reward-filled entry into the **heavenly** realm, where they become the *bride* of Christ and enter *heaven itself* (Revelation 19:7–9; 21:2).

On the other hand, those of **non-elect salvation** may not be the bride, but part of the **nations of those who are saved** (Revelation 21:24). These do not enter heaven but dwell on the **new earth**. As stated in **1 Corinthians 15:40**, resurrection bodies may differ—celestial for the elect and terrestrial for others. Thus, all Christians may enter heaven, while many others, though saved, may be confined to the earth.

Such distinctions, if grounded in Scripture, reveal that salvation itself may occur in degrees, and that mercy in the afterlife, though rare and conditional, remains a theological possibility acknowledged both in ancient testimony and consistent with literal biblical language.

CHAPTER 5 Does the "Thief in the Night" Phrase Refer to a Secret Coming of Christ?

INTRODUCTION

The Pentecostal movement popularized the doctrine of a secret coming of Christ through what is now known as the "secret rapture." This concept was first systematized by John Nelson Darby (1800–1882), a preacher within the Plymouth Brethren movement. Despite modern enthusiasm for this theory, there is a striking lack of concrete evidence that any early church group ever treated this as an article of faith. The idea does not appear in the creeds, confessions, or catechisms of the ancient church. It is an innovation that only gained traction during the 19th century.

This essay focuses on the phrase "thief in the night" by examining its biblical usage and the writings of early Chiliasm-supporting Church Fathers. The purpose is to demonstrate that Scripture consistently teaches a singular, public, and visible second coming of Christ. If this conclusion is correct, then the secret rapture theory is not only unbiblical but potentially dangerous. Those who believe in a pre-tribulation escape may become spiritually complacent, failing to prepare for the trials associated with the final antichrist and the great tribulation.

A right understanding of the coming of Christ guards against breaking the third commandment—taking the Name of Jehovah in vain—by avoiding speculative or inaccurate prophetic claims. A biblical examination of this subject will help believers discern which voices they ought to trust when it comes to interpreting prophecy.

PRE TRIBULATION RAPTURE CLAIMS IN ANTIQUITY

Some modern writers claim the pre-tribulation rapture was taught in the early church and later lost. One of their primary arguments is based on the language of imminency found in Scripture. However, phrases denoting imminency are not exclusive to eschatology. For example, in Revelation 3:3, Christ speaks of coming "like a thief" to the first-century church at Sardis—a warning clearly about judgment for lack of repentance, not an eschatological rapture. Pre-tribulation advocates attempt to stretch the future tense in that passage to support a dual fulfillment idea, but this interpretation makes little sense if one considers that no such event ever occurred for Sardis.

Another passage often quoted is from the *Shepherd of Hermas*, which speaks of "escaping the great tribulation." But a careful reading reveals that this escape refers not to avoidance of tribulation but perseverance through it.

> "Happy you who endure the great tribulation that is coming on… These then are to deny Him in the days that are coming. To those who denied in earlier times, God became gracious, on account of His exceeding tender mercy."

The meaning of "escape" here clearly involves enduring, not avoiding, the tribulation. The fire that tests them purifies the elect, just as gold is refined by fire. This is an endurance-based salvation, not an evacuation from danger.

> "Those, therefore, who continue steadfast, and are put through the fire, will be purified by means of it... This then is the type of the great tribulation that is to come."

The vision presents no two-tiered elect group in which some undergo tribulation while others escape. Rather, all of the elect are refined by it.

Another document often cited is *The Sermon on the Last Times, the Antichrist, and the End of the World*, commonly known as *Pseudo-Ephraem*. This sermon contains the phrase:

> "For all the saints and elect of God are gathered, prior to the tribulation that is to come, and are taken to the Lord lest they see the confusion that is to overwhelm the world because of our sins" (section 2).

Pre-tribulationists interpret this as support for a secret rapture. However, the statement that "all the saints and elect" are gathered is problematic for that view. Pre-trib doctrine teaches that only some believers are raptured while others (the so-called "left behind") endure the final seven-year tribulation. If all are taken, then no believers should remain on earth. Yet this same text describes Christians enduring the tribulation.

> "In those days people shall not be buried, neither Christian, nor heretic, neither Jew, nor pagan... because all people, while they are fleeing, ignore them" (section 4).

This indicates that Christians remain present during the horrors described, which contradicts the earlier claim—unless the gathering refers not to an early rapture, but to the public second coming of Christ. Other references in *Pseudo-Ephraem* confirm that believers endure the tribulation.

> "In these three years and a half... there will be a great tribulation... But those who wander through the deserts... bend their knees to God... and are sustained by the salvation of the Lord" (section 8).

These are the faithful who survive through the fire, not escape it.

Section 9 reinforces this by describing the arrival of Elijah and Enoch as prophetic witnesses during the antichrist's reign. These figures exhort the "faithful witnesses to God" during the time of great deception, a further proof that true believers remain on earth:

> "...he sends to them consolatory proclamation by his attendants, the prophets Enoch and Elijah... and they call back the faithful witnesses to God."

Finally, section 10 of the same sermon reveals that the coming of Christ occurs "after the resurrection of the two prophets" and after the "three and a half years have been completed." The Son of Man appears publicly with angelic trumpets and the sign of the cross—clearly describing the public second coming, not a secret rapture.

> "And when the three and a half years have been completed... will come the sign of the Son of Man... the angelic trumpet precedes him... Then Christ shall come and the enemy shall be thrown into confusion."

This public event matches the second coming described in Matthew 24:29–31 and 2 Thessalonians 1:7–10, not a secret disappearance. The gathering of "all the saints and elect" mentioned in section 2 must refer to this final coming, not a hidden escape.

Thus, any notion that *Pseudo-Ephraem* teaches a secret, pre-tribulation rapture is unfounded. The evidence in the sermon itself makes clear that believers are present and active during the tribulation. The only deliverance they experience is at the moment of Christ's final return.

POST TRIBULATION RAPTURE BELIEF IN KEY SCHOLARS OF THE CHURCH

All scholars in earlier church history believed in a post-tribulation rapture. That is, they did not believe in a secret coming of Christ via a pre-tribulation rapture theory. The consistent testimony across early Christian writings is that the Church will be persecuted by the Antichrist rather than escaping that tribulation. No early Christian writings suggest that any portion of the Church is taken away before this final tribulation. Here are some representative quotes:

> "... the kingdom of Antichrist shall fiercely, though for a short time, assail the Church before the last judgment of God" (Augustine of Hippo, c.354–430).

> "He [Christ] shall come from heaven with glory, when the man of apostasy, who speaks strange things against the Most High, shall venture to do unlawful deeds on the earth against us the Christians" (Justin of Rome, c.100–165).

> "... and that he shall be himself the eighth among them. And they shall lay Babylon waste, and burn her with fire, and shall give their kingdom to the beast, and put the Church to flight. After that they shall be destroyed by the coming of our Lord" (Irenaeus of Lyons, c.130–202).

> "... the beast Antichrist with his false prophet may wage war on the Church of God" (Tertullian, c.155–220).

> "That refers to the one thousand two hundred and threescore days (the half of the week) during which the tyrant is to reign and persecute the Church" (Hippolytus of Rome, c.170–235).

> "... that the day of affliction has begun to hang over our heads, and the end of the world and the time of Antichrist to draw near, so that we must all stand prepared for the battle" (Cyprian of Carthage, c.210–258).

> "... the times of Antichrist, when there shall be a great famine, and when all shall be injured ... He speaks of Elias the prophet, who is the precursor of the times of Antichrist, for the restoration and establishment of the churches from the great and intolerable persecution" (Victorinus of Pettau, died c.303).

"Then he [Antichrist] will attempt to destroy the temple of God, and persecute the righteous people; and there will be distress and tribulation, such as there never has been from the beginning of the world. ... When these things shall so happen, then the righteous and the followers of truth shall separate themselves from the wicked, and flee into solitudes" (Lactantius, c.250–325).

"We preach not one advent only of Christ, but a second also, far more glorious than the former. ... In His first coming, He endured the Cross, despising shame (Hebrews 12:2); in His second, He comes attended by a host of Angels, receiving glory. ... The Church now charges you before the Living God; she declares to you the things concerning Antichrist before they arrive. Whether they will happen in your time we know not, or whether they will happen after you we know not; but it is well that, knowing these things, you should make yourself secure beforehand. ... As though he [Antichrist] were the expected Christ, he shall afterwards be characterized by all kinds of crimes of inhumanity and lawlessness, so as to outdo all unrighteous and ungodly men who have gone before him; displaying against all men, but especially against us Christians, a spirit murderous and most cruel, merciless and crafty. And after perpetrating such things for three years and six months only, he shall be destroyed by the glorious second advent from heaven of the only-begotten Son of God, our Lord and Saviour Jesus, the true Christ, who shall slay Antichrist with the breath of His mouth, and shall deliver him over to the fire of hell" (Cyril of Jerusalem, c.313–386).

It is worth noting that even the key founders of the Protestant churches after the Reformation also held firmly to a post-tribulation rapture view. They affirmed that the Church must undergo this final dreadful tribulation, again with no mention of a secret rapture rescuing any portion of the faithful beforehand.

"... the work of St. John, the Apostle, or of whomever else ... Since it is intended as a revelation of things that are to happen in the future, and especially of tribulations and disasters for the Church" (Martin Luther, 1483–1546).

"Though all the heresies and schisms which have existed from the beginning belong to the kingdom of Antichrist, yet when Paul predicts an approaching apostasy, he signifies by this description that that seat of abomination shall then be erected, when a universal defection shall have seized the Church ... this is the principal indication which we ought to follow in our inquiries after Antichrist, especially where such pride proceeds to a public desolation of the Church" (John Calvin, 1509–1564).

"21. Then shall be great tribulation—Have not many things spoken in the chapter, as well as in Mark 13 and Luke 21, a farther and much more extensive meaning than has been yet fulfilled? 22. And unless those days were shortened—By the taking of Jerusalem sooner than could be expected: No flesh would be saved—The whole nation would be destroyed. But for the elect's sake—That is, for the sake of the Christians. ... 29. Immediately after the tribulation of those days—Here our Lord begins to speak of His last coming" (John Wesley, 1703–1791).

TESTIMONY OF CHILIASM CHURCH FATHERS

Since "no prophecy of Scripture is of any private interpretation" (2 Peter 1:20), it is both reasonable and necessary to examine the surviving writings from the earliest era of Christianity—particularly the Chiliasm church fathers. These men are often among the most reliable voices in matters of eschatological interpretation. By "Chiliasm fathers," we specifically refer to three foundational theologians: Justin of Rome (also known as Justin Martyr), Irenaeus of Lyons, and Tertullian.

These men taught that Christ would come twice—once in humiliation (past), and once in glory (future). This consistent framework of two advents stands in direct opposition to any secret or intermediate coming of Christ. Thus, the "thief in the night" phrase must refer to the one and only future public second coming of Christ, since there is no third or secret coming described in these ancient sources.

Justin of Rome writes:

"For the prophets have proclaimed two advents of His: the one, that which is already past, when He came as a dishonoured and suffering Man; but the second, when, according to prophecy, He shall come from heaven with glory, accompanied by His angelic host, when also He shall raise the bodies of all men who have lived, and shall clothe those of the worthy with immortality, and shall send those of the wicked, endued with eternal sensibility, into everlasting fire with the wicked devils. And that these things also have been foretold as yet to be, we will prove."

Irenaeus of Lyons concurs:

"... and do not recognise the advent of Christ, which He accomplished for the salvation of men, nor are willing to understand that all the prophets announced His two advents: the one, indeed, in which He became a man subject to stripes, and knowing what it is to bear infirmity (Isaiah 53:3) ... but the second in which He will come on the clouds (Daniel 7:13), bringing on the day which burns as a furnace (Malachi 4:1), and smiting the earth with the word of His mouth (Isaiah 11:4), and slaying the impious with the breath of His lips, and having a fan in His hands, and cleansing His floor, and gathering the wheat indeed into His barn, but burning the chaff with unquenchable fire (Matthew 3:12; Luke 3:17)."

Tertullian's writings go a step further by explicitly using the phrase "thief in the night" in reference to Christ's second coming. His quote, which will be examined in the next section, affirms that this phrase was not applied to any secret coming, but to the very public and glorious return of the Lord in judgment.

THIEF IN THE NIGHT PHRASE

When the relevant Bible verses are read literally, we observe that the phrase "I am coming as a thief" is stated **after** the sixth angel has poured out his bowl of God's wrath. This timing makes clear that the "thief in the night" coming has not occurred **up to that point**, meaning it takes place very late— near the end of the antichrist's reign. This reading supports the post-tribulation rapture position. Pre-tribulation scholars, however, attempt to interpret the thief phrase symbolically. Some claim it refers only to Armageddon, while others suggest it speaks of unbelievers' spiritual unawareness after the rapture has already happened.

Scripture says:

"So the first went and poured out his bowl upon the earth, and a foul and loathsome sore came upon the men who had the mark of the beast and those who worshiped his image. ... Then the sixth angel poured out his bowl on the great river Euphrates, and its water was dried up, so that the way of the kings from the east might be prepared. And I saw three unclean spirits like frogs coming out of the mouth of the dragon, out of the mouth of the beast, and out of the mouth of the false prophet. For they are spirits of demons, performing signs, which go out to the kings of the earth and of the whole world, to gather them to the battle of that great day of God Almighty. **"Behold, I am coming as a thief. Blessed is he who watches, and keeps his garments, lest he walk naked and they see his shame."** And they gathered them together to the place called in Hebrew, Armageddon" (Revelation 16:2, 12–16).

The problem with the pre-tribulation allegorical interpretation is that this thief reference directly describes a **blessed** group—those who watch and keep their garments. This cannot refer to unbelievers, who by definition are not "watching." And if the faithful watchers were already raptured earlier, why is Christ still issuing the command to watch at this late stage, just before Armageddon?

Furthermore, if the phrase "thief in the night" is applied both to a supposed secret coming and to a public event, then it ceases to carry its alleged distinction. The pre-tribulation interpretation collapses under its own logic. The entire defense of a secret rapture rests on the "thief" imagery referring **only** to something unexpected and invisible. Yet, Christ Himself utters this phrase **after** the sixth bowl, making it anything but secret or early.

Revelation 13 establishes that the mark of the beast and the beast's 42-month authority occur **before** this thief statement is uttered. Thus, the secret pre- or mid-tribulational rapture theory is rendered untenable, for Christ's warning clearly comes **after** the final antichrist's rise and reign.

> "And I saw one of his heads as if it had been mortally wounded, and his deadly wound was healed. And all the world marveled and followed the beast. So they worshiped the dragon who gave authority to the beast; and they worshiped the beast, saying, 'Who is like the beast? Who is able to make war with him?' And he was given a mouth speaking great things and blasphemies, and he was given authority to continue for forty-two months… He causes all, both small and great, rich and poor, free and slave, to receive a mark on their right hand or on their foreheads… and that no one may buy or sell except one who has the mark or the name of the beast, or the number of his name… His number is 666" (Revelation 13:3–5, 16–18).

Post-tribulation scholars also interpret all "thief in the night" references in the New Testament as pointing to the **same** second coming of Christ. Even where imminency is emphasized—such as not knowing the exact day or hour—it does not demand multiple comings. It simply means believers must remain vigilant during tribulation, knowing deliverance will come suddenly but **after** the great affliction.

Jesus said:

> "But of that day and hour no one knows, not even the angels of heaven, but My Father only. But as the days of Noah were, so also will the coming of the Son of Man be... They did not know until the flood came and took them all away, so also will the coming of the Son of Man be... Watch therefore, for you do not know what hour your Lord is coming. But know this, that if the master of the house had known what hour the thief would come, he would have watched... Therefore you also be ready, for the Son of Man is coming at an hour you do not expect" (Matthew 24:36–44).

Peter affirms this same meaning in his epistle:

> "But the day of the Lord will come as a thief in the night, in which the heavens will pass away with a great noise, and the elements will melt with fervent heat; both the earth and the works that are in it will be burned up" (2 Peter 3:10).

This verse clearly involves **noise, fire**, and **global upheaval**—not secrecy or invisibility. The destruction of the old world and preparation for the millennial reign of Christ fits the Chiliasm timeline. Zechariah confirms that mortal nations will still exist and be held accountable during the millennial age:

> "And it shall come to pass that everyone who is left of all the nations which came against Jerusalem shall go up from year to year to worship the King, the Lord of hosts, and to keep the Feast of Tabernacles... If the family of Egypt will not come up and enter in, they shall have no rain... This shall be the punishment... that do not come up to keep the Feast of Tabernacles" (Zechariah 14:16–19).

Even Christ's message to Sardis includes "thief" language as a warning to **believers**, not unbelievers:

> "Be watchful, and strengthen the things which remain... I have not found your works perfect before God... If you will not watch, I will come upon you as a thief, and you will not know what hour I will come upon you" (Revelation 3:2–3).

This rebuke is clearly **not** a reference to a literal second coming to Sardis in the first century, but rather a figurative warning about spiritual readiness.

Nevertheless, it supports the consistent theme: Christ's coming will be **sudden**, and only those who are watchful and faithful will be ready.

Tertullian, a primary source among the Chiliasm fathers, likewise connects all the "thief" language with the **public** second coming, after the antichrist is revealed:

> "For you yourselves know perfectly, that the day of the Lord comes as a thief in the night… That day shall not come, unless indeed there first come a falling away… and that man of sin be revealed… Even him whose coming is after the working of Satan… whom the Lord shall consume with the spirit of His mouth, and shall destroy with the brightness of His coming" (1 Thessalonians 5:1–3; 2 Thessalonians 2:1–10, as quoted by Tertullian).

There is no bifurcation here between a secret rapture and a public return. Tertullian treats these prophecies as **one event**, consistent with the other early fathers.

CONCLUSION

There is no historical or theological proof from the Chiliasm church fathers for a secret pre-tribulation coming of Christ. No quote links any "thief in the night" reference to a hidden rapture. Rather, all such references consistently align with a **single, visible, post-tribulation** second coming— after the rise and terror of the final antichrist.

Even 1 Thessalonians 4:17, often quoted to support pre-tribulation rapture, was understood by early Christians as part of that same public coming. Not one ancient writer separates the "gathering" of the saints from the destruction of the antichrist.

The post-tribulation view therefore stands not only on solid Scriptural ground but also on the unified testimony of the early church. The phrase "thief in the night," when properly interpreted in its biblical context and confirmed by the historical witness of the fathers, points only to one glorious and climactic return of Christ, visible to all, and occurring **after** the great tribulation.

CHAPTER 6 Non-Elect Salvation Possibility via Saved by Fire

SAVED BY FIRE

Let us examine 1 Corinthians 3:15. Protestants generally interpret the phrase "saved by fire" as referring to a believer who undergoes fiery trials in this life, yet is ultimately saved prior to death. This interpretation remains confined to the living Christian's experience, often understood as a metaphor for the testing of one's faith and works. Roman Catholics, by contrast, understand this passage in light of their doctrine of purgatory, applying it to an imperfect catechumen who is purified post-mortem before entering heaven.

A third interpretation arises when we consider the possibility of **non-elect salvation**. In this view, 1 Corinthians 3:15 may refer to someone **not** identified as a Christian. The distinction becomes clear when this verse is compared with verse 14: "If anyone's work which he has built on it endures, he will receive a reward." A Christian, whose faith is alive, produces living works and thus is rewarded with the **inheritance** (Colossians 3:24), corresponding with the promise of verse 14. In contrast, verse 15 explicitly says that this person "will suffer loss"—a phrase that clearly implies **no reward**, although salvation is still granted.

If both verse 14 and verse 15 described the same class of believers with the same outcome, then there would be no real contrast between them. Yet the text makes that contrast central. The individual in verse 15 is saved **"yet so as through fire,"** indicating a salvific process distinct from the reward-based salvation of the faithful Christian.

When correlated with the Parable of the Sower (Matthew 13:8, 23), the good ground refers to Christians who produce a harvest of thirty, sixty, or even a hundredfold. This points to spiritual productivity rewarded in heaven. It would be inconsistent to associate the "saved by fire" individual—who has **no reward**—with those who produce even the minimum fruit of thirtyfold.

Such a person may not undergo afterlife judgment like the wicked, yet their salvation is through fire and void of reward, marking a distinct category.

This raises a critical question: If this is not the elect, what kind of salvation is this?

The answer may lie in understanding the distinction between the **elect** and the **non-elect**. The elect are granted **celestial (heavenly)** resurrection bodies suited for entry into heaven itself. The non-elect, by contrast, may be raised with **terrestrial (earthly)** bodies (1 Corinthians 15:40), which still bear glory but are of a lesser kind—perhaps suitable only for the renewed earth.

This interpretation aligns with Revelation 21. In that chapter, the **bride**—clearly symbolic of the elect—descends from heaven (Revelation 21:2, 9–10). The **nations of those who are saved** are mentioned separately (Revelation 21:24), which implies a distinction. This is after the book of life has already been revealed (Revelation 21:27), meaning the great white throne judgment (Revelation 20:11–15) is past. If some of the saved nations **are not** included among the bride, then they must constitute another class of the redeemed: the non-elect.

All Christians are identified in Scripture as **kings and priests** (Revelation 1:6; 5:10), and the early church fathers affirm this interpretation. The bride therefore must be composed of those who fulfill this kingly-priestly role. Revelation 21:24 says, "And the kings of the earth bring their glory and honor into it." If these kings are the bride, then those they rule over—these nations of the saved—may represent the non-elect. These nations are only allowed to dwell on the **new earth**, not necessarily enter the **lowest heaven** that connects to it (Revelation 21:1–2, 10).

Those not found in the book of life are cast into the **lake of fire** (Revelation 20:15). However, 1 Corinthians 3:15 opens the possibility that **some** may be "saved by fire" **after** being cast into this final punishment. This suggests **two distinct classes** among the condemned: those who suffer the **second death permanently**, and those who, though hurt by it, are eventually restored. This may explain why some from the saved nations require the **leaves of the tree of life for healing** (Revelation 22:2)—having been harmed by the fire but not utterly destroyed.

Perhaps this healing process is the only way their **terrestrial bodies** can receive sustaining life from Christ, just as the elect will be raised to reign for 1,000 years in human flesh during the millennial reign (Revelation 20:4–6). In Genesis, God prevented access to the tree of life in the fallen state (Genesis 3:22–24), lest man live forever in sin. In contrast, after the judgment, access to the tree is granted to those whose names are written in the book of life—yet some require its healing properties, implying previous damage or limitation, perhaps consistent with being "saved by fire."

The elect alone experience a **change** from human (terrestrial) to **angelic (celestial)** nature at the end of the millennium. As Paul states, "flesh and blood cannot inherit the kingdom of God" (1 Corinthians 15:50–52). This transformation culminates in the Christian's union with Christ at the **marriage of the Lamb** (Revelation 19:7–9), where they become truly "one flesh" with Him in resurrection glory.

This truth was affirmed by the early church. **Irenaeus of Lyons** and **Tertullian** both testify that believers must first live out their rewards in the millennial kingdom—still in mortal flesh—before undergoing the transformation to immortality. The body of the Christian is recompensed on the renewed earth with sinless pleasures and full inheritance before being glorified into a body "no longer of flesh and blood."

In contrast, the non-elect, having passed through fire, may receive life on the new earth, healed but **not transformed** into the heavenly image. They partake of God's mercy, yet not of the full inheritance.

SHEPHERD OF HERMAS

Did early Christians hold a distinction between elect salvation and non-elect salvation in the way outlined here? One of the clearest examples suggesting such a framework appears in the *Shepherd of Hermas*, a Christian text widely read and even regarded by some early churches as Scripture or nearly Scriptural. This writing provides one of the earliest illustrations of what could be described as an elect salvation (symbolized by the tower) in contrast with a separate, more inferior form of salvation after judgment (outside the tower).

In *The Shepherd*, the tower metaphor represents the elect Church. Those who are part of this tower are described as stones, carefully selected and perfectly placed. This imagery appears in the following passage:

> "Many indeed shall hear, and hearing, some shall be glad, and some shall weep. But even these, if they hear and repent, shall also rejoice. Hear, then, the parables of the tower... The tower which you see building is myself, the Church, who have appeared to you now and on the former occasion. Ask, then, whatever you like in regard to the tower, and I will reveal it to you, that you may rejoice with the saints."

This interpretation of the elect as stones in the tower was later affirmed by **Irenaeus**, indicating that this reading was part of early Christian consensus. However, *The Shepherd* goes further by presenting a group of people who, though initially rejected as unfit for the tower, are nonetheless eventually saved—but only **after judgment and torment**. This seems to indicate a category of salvation distinct from the elect, possibly aligning with the non-elect salvation discussed in 1 Corinthians 3:15.

The relevant passage reads:

> "Do you wish to know who are the others which fell near the waters, but could not be rolled into them? These are they who have heard the word and wish to be baptized in the name of the Lord; but when the chastity demanded by the truth comes into their recollection, they draw back, and again walk after their own wicked desires. She finished her exposition of the tower. But I, shameless as I yet was, asked her, Is repentance possible for all those stones which have been cast away and did not fit into the building of the tower, and will they yet have a place in this tower? Repentance, said she, is yet possible, but in this tower, they cannot find a suitable place. But in another and much inferior place they will be laid, and that, too, only when they have been tortured and completed the days of their sins. And on this account will they be transferred, because they have partaken of the righteous Word. And then only will they be removed from their punishments when the thought of repenting of the evil deeds which they have done has come into their hearts. But if it does not come into their hearts, they will not be saved on account of the hardness of their heart."

Some Roman Catholic interpreters use this passage in support of the purgatory doctrine. However, the language of the Shepherd more strongly points to a group **outside** the tower, not inside it. In Roman Catholicism, purgatory is viewed as a chamber of purifying punishment for those destined for heaven—thus still inside the elect sphere. But the Shepherd of Hermas makes it clear that these rejected stones "will be laid" in a "much inferior place" which **is not the tower**. This seems to imply a **completely distinct location**, not just a lesser level within the elect's eternal dwelling.

By comparison, the **tower**—as a symbol of the elect—can be seen as corresponding to the final new heaven. In contrast, the **inferior place** assigned to those judged and purified later might correspond to the **new earth**, where nations are saved but clearly remain outside the heavenly city (Revelation 21:24, 27). These outsiders are not permitted to enter the heavenly Jerusalem, where it is said of the elect that "they shall go out no more" (Revelation 3:12). That language underscores a permanent residence in heaven for the elect, distinguishing them from other saved persons.

This view also aligns with a fragment preserved by **Papias**, an early chiliasm teacher, who articulated a tiered view of eternal reward. His quote affirms a distinction among three groups of saved individuals:

> "As the presbyters say, then those who are deemed worthy of an abode in heaven shall go there, others shall enjoy the delights of Paradise, and others shall possess the splendour of the city; for everywhere the Saviour will be seen, according as they shall be worthy who see Him. But that there is this distinction between the habitation of those who produce an hundredfold, and that of those who produce sixty-fold, and that of those who produce thirty-fold; for the first will be taken up into the heavens, the second class will dwell in Paradise, and the last will inhabit the city."

In this framework, **all three categories are saved**, yet only the most faithful reach the heavens. The rest remain either in Paradise or the city—perhaps corresponding to varying levels of reward and intimacy with Christ. It is significant that **all three are described as Christian categories** in this passage, reinforcing the idea that reward is tied to fruitfulness (Matthew 13:8).

Further support for this understanding is provided by **Irenaeus**, who affirms a similar layered structure of final abodes. He draws directly from Isaiah and other Old Testament prophecies to confirm a lasting distinction between heavenly and earthly realms after the new creation. His quote reads:

> "But when this [present] fashion [of things] passes away, and man has been renewed, and flourishes in an incorruptible state, so as to preclude the possibility of becoming old, [then] there shall be the new heaven and the new earth, in which the new man shall remain [continually], always holding fresh converse with God. And as the presbyters say, Then those who are deemed worthy of an abode in heaven shall go there, others shall enjoy the delights of paradise, and others shall possess the splendour of the city; for everywhere the Saviour shall be seen according as they who see Him shall be worthy."

While Irenaeus does affirm that all these categories are part of the renewed creation, his phrasing suggests that only the **worthy ones** enter the heavenly realms. By implication, those who are unworthy but still saved might remain confined to the **earthly domain**. This again aligns with the

Shepherd's imagery of those who, after judgment and punishment, are placed in an inferior location—not among the stones of the tower.

The convergence of these sources—*The Shepherd of Hermas*, Papias, and Irenaeus—strongly indicates that **early Christians** may have viewed salvation as **multifaceted**, distinguishing between an **elect salvation** associated with the heavens and a possible **non-elect salvation** outside the elect structure, potentially located on the new earth.

CONCLUSION

Non-elect salvation may refer to those distinct from the "few" who attain elect salvation. The elect become Christ's bride and inherit heaven itself, as promised to the overcomers. By contrast, non-elect salvation refers to those whose final abode is not in heaven, but on the renewed earth. These individuals are saved not by personal merit or prior faith, but through Christ's ransom for "many," possibly having come to belief after seeing Him in the spirit world.

This framework may help illuminate the structure of the penultimate chapter of the Bible, which appears to distinguish three categories of people:

i) **The Overcomers / Christians / Elect Salvation** – These are those with faith who inherit all things:

"He who overcomes shall inherit all things, and I will be his God and he shall be My son." (Revelation 21:7)

ii) **The Thirsty / Non-Christians / Non-Elect Salvation** – These are those without faith or reward, who are saved by God's mercy through fire:

"I will give of the fountain of the water of life freely to him who thirsts." (Revelation 21:6)

iii) **The Damned / Unsaved Non-Christians / The Wicked** – These are eternally condemned:

"But the cowardly, unbelieving, abominable, murderers, sexually immoral, sorcerers, idolaters, and all liars shall have their part in the lake which burns with fire and brimstone, which is the second death." (Revelation 21:8)

The final chapter of the Apocalypse may also reflect these threefold distinctions:

i) **Elect Salvation – the Bride** – Those who participated in the wedding of the Lamb and the first resurrection (cf. Matthew 25:1–13):

> "And the Spirit and the bride say, 'Come!'" (Revelation 22:17)

ii) **Non-Elect Salvation – Israel (the Servants)** – Those who serve before the throne, possibly referring to faithful Israelites (cf. Matthew 25:14–30):

> "And there shall be no more curse, but the throne of God and of the Lamb shall be in it, and His servants shall serve Him. They shall see His face, and His name shall be on their foreheads." (Revelation 22:3–4)

iii) **Non-Elect Salvation – Gentiles (the Thirsty)** – Those among the nations who are saved, not as part of the bride, but by the free offer of the water of life (cf. Matthew 25:31–46):

> "And let him who thirsts come. Whoever desires, let him take the water of life freely." (Revelation 22:17)

The academic idea of **Non-Elect Salvation** is relatively recent, grounded in theological inquiry rather than established doctrine. It does not claim certainty, and should therefore be approached with scholarly caution. However, the interpretive framework aligns literally with various biblical texts. As such, it merits honest theological consideration—not as dogma, but as a viable possibility consistent with the plain reading of Scripture.

CHAPTER 7 Prophecy of 5 Wise and 5 Foolish Virgins in Chiliasm

INTRODUCTION

The parable of the five wise and five foolish virgins spoken by the Lord Jesus Christ (Matthew 25:1–13) is important because it directly pertains to elect salvation and the privilege of participating in the wedding of the Lamb. Throughout ancient Christianity and the subsequent centuries, this parable has been understood as referring to those who both believe in Christ and practice good works. This interpretation is affirmed in the formal creeds and teachings of both the Catholic and Orthodox churches.

The shared consensus across traditions is that "it is important to observe that this entire discourse is concerned with practicing and keeping that which has been commanded by Jesus." However, each church or denomination varies in the particular commands of Christ they emphasize as necessary for salvation.

During the Reformation, this foundational idea remained intact but with greater emphasis placed on correct doctrine and fidelity to Scripture as the supreme authority. This focus is often summarized in what became known as the Five Solas: *sola scriptura* (Scripture alone), *solus Christus* (Christ alone), *sola fide* (faith alone), *sola gratia* (grace alone), and *soli Deo gloria* (glory to God alone). These principles became central to the Reformation tradition's effort to align the teachings of the early church fathers with the plain reading of Scripture.

The Reformers also strongly contended that the Catholic and Orthodox churches were in error, and in some cases even unsaved, due to their extra-biblical doctrines and practices—such as the veneration or invocation of Mary and the saints, and their view that justification involves sacramental works. In response, the Catholic and Orthodox churches anathematized the Reformers and Protestants, asserting that their doctrinal deviations removed them from the true church.

In the early 20th century, a new religious movement emerged called the Pentecostal revival, claiming itself to be the true end-time church. Notably, Pentecostal leaders such as William Seymour (1870–1922) advanced a novel interpretation of the parable of the wise and foolish virgins. According to this view, the wise virgins are Pentecostals who have received a double portion of the Holy Spirit, evidenced by speaking in tongues. This belief system began during the Azusa Street Revival, where it was taught that glossolalia in a non-human language was the biblical proof of having the Spirit. Those who did not speak in tongues were said to be without the Spirit and, consequently, unprepared for Christ's return. They argued that only such Pentecostals would be taken in a secret rapture before the great tribulation under the final antichrist.

The fundamental problem with this view, however, is that there is no record of such a teaching for the first 1900 years of Christian history. Post-tribulationists often point this out, noting that no church father or early Christian document makes this connection between tongues-speaking and the parable of the virgins. The novelty of the interpretation stands in contrast to the continuity of historic Christian exegesis, especially within the chiliasm framework.

REFORMERS

Martin Luther (1483–1546), the founder of the Lutheran churches, taught that the phrase "five are wise, five foolish" applies to all Christians, whom Christ collectively calls "virgins." He emphasized that true faith includes both inward belief and outward practice, especially seen in acts of mercy toward one's neighbor. The foolish, by contrast, profess faith but remain unchanged in their character and behavior—still covetous, unmerciful, and selfish.

He writes:

> "Now pay attention: this parable speaks of the time right before the Last Judgment of God, and thus it applies to all Christians. For many of them—the majority—will turn, some to the imaginary faith, and the others to the true faith. ... To expand further on the Gospel, notice that the lamps are intended to depict for us an outward thing and a bodily practice. But the lamps together with the oil are the inner treasures with the true faith. ... Five are wise, five foolish. Here He calls all Christians 'virgins.' ... Matthew writes (7:22), saying: 'Lord, Lord!' The mouth is there, but the heart is far away (Matt. 15:8). The oil is not in the lamp,

that is, faith is not in the heart. They give it no thought. Indeed, they know it not and imagine that their lamps are ready. Their nature is that they gladly hear the preaching about faith, and if they have heard the Word, they invent and fabricate for themselves a thought, a delusion in the heart which they consider to be oil, and yet they remain the same as before in their behavior. Following their old ways, they are just as wrathful as before, just as covetous, just as unmerciful toward the poor, just as discourteous, etc. … Therefore, let each one see to it that he has these two together: the oil, which is true faith and trust in Christ; and the lamps, the vessel, which is the outward service toward your neighbor. The whole Christian life consists in these two things: Believe God. Help your neighbor. The whole Gospel teaches this. Parents should tell it to their children at home and everywhere. Children, too, should constantly foster this Word among themselves."

John Calvin (1509–1564), founder of the Reformed churches and the namesake of Calvinism, gave a similar interpretation. He explained that the parable portrays true belief as bearing fruit in charity, which he defined as believers giving mutual aid to one another. This cooperation stems from the diverse gifts God has distributed among His people, to be used for the benefit of the whole church.

He writes:

"But I take it more simply as denoting earthly occupations, in which believers must be engaged, so long as they dwell in the body; and, though forgetfulness of the kingdom of God ought never to steal upon them, yet the distracting influence of the occupations of this world is not inappropriately compared to sleep. For they cannot be so constantly occupied with the thought of meeting Christ, as not to be distracted, or retarded, or entangled by a variety of cares, in consequence of which, while they watch, they are partly asleep. … 9. Lest there be not enough for you and us. We know that the Lord distributes His gifts so variously to each, according to his measure, in order that they may give mutual aid to each other, and may employ for the general advantage what has been entrusted to each individual; and that in this way is preserved the sacred connection which exists among the members of the Church. … There is no other way of obtaining it, therefore, but to receive by faith what is offered to us."

John Wesley (1703–1791), the key founder of the Methodist churches, summarized the lamp as faith and the oil as love—thus viewing their combination as "faith working by love." His emphasis was not merely on doctrinal belief, but on the application of faith through love-driven deeds.

He writes:

"1: Then shall the kingdom of heaven—that is, the candidates for it—be like ten virgins. The bridemaids on the wedding night were wont to go to the house where the bride was, with burning lamps or torches in their hands, to wait for the bridegroom's coming. When he drew near, they went to meet him with their lamps, and to conduct him to the bride. 3: The foolish took no oil with them—no more than kept them burning just for the present. None to supply their future want, to recruit their lamp's decay. The lamp is faith. A lamp and oil with it, is faith working by love. 4: The wise took oil in their vessels—love in their hearts. And they daily sought a fresh supply of spiritual strength, till their faith was made perfect."

Wesley strongly emphasized the practice of financial holiness—a term suitable to denote obedience to Christ's commands relating to the use of wealth. He taught that increasing wealth without proportionate increase in giving may lead even believers into judgment. He warned that money can become a snare unless used in charity doctrine, specifically through sacrificial almsgiving.

He writes:

"For the Methodists in every place grow diligent and frugal; consequently they increase in goods. Hence, they proportionably increase in pride, in the desire of the flesh, the desire of the eyes, and the pride of life. So, although the form of religion remains, the spirit is swiftly vanishing away. Is there no way to prevent this?—this continual declension of pure religion? We ought not to forbid people to be diligent and frugal; we must exhort all Christians to gain all they can, and to save all they can: this is, in effect, to grow rich! What way then, I ask again, can we take that our money may not sink us to the nethermost hell? There is one way, and there is no other under heaven. If those who gain all they can, and save all they can, will likewise give all they can, then the more they gain, the more they will grow in grace, and the more treasure they will lay up in heaven."

This view reflects the teaching of the Chiliasm church fathers presented next: that pure religion must involve both holiness in the form of sin-avoidance and charity expressed in proportion to one's means. This "relative measure" of giving is demonstrated by tangible acts of love—especially to those in need, beginning with the widows and orphans, as James writes:

> "Pure religion and undefiled before God and the Father is this, To visit the fatherless and widows in their affliction, and to keep himself unspotted from the world."

Relative measure means that those unable to give—such as the extremely poor, the sick, or those receiving aid themselves—may be exempt. Lazarus is a prime example. His poverty exempted him from such works, and both Irenaeus and Tertullian understood this account as referring to a real person.

Even Christian widows who received financial help from the church were expected to have lived a life of charity doctrine beforehand, such as raising children, lodging strangers, and relieving the afflicted. Tabitha is explicitly called a "disciple" and described as "full of good works and charitable deeds."

Men, being leaders, are required to do even more. Paul commands the rich to be "rich in good works, ready to give, willing to share" (1 Timothy 6:18), which is financial holiness, contributing to sanctification that leads to eternal life (1 Timothy 6:19).

Thus, the Reformers—like the Chiliasm church fathers—affirmed that faith must be living. It must be expressed not only by belief but also by works of love, particularly toward those in need. That is the heart of what Christ commended in the wise virgins.

HOLINESS AND CHARITY DOCTRINE

Firstly, Irenaeus of Lyons (c. 130–c. 202) warned that those who obscure the interpretation of the parables may not be among those of elect salvation, being "excluded from His marriage-chamber." This is why it is vital to take the Chiliasm prophecy and doctrine quotes seriously. If any interpolation is made, it should be supported by at least one or more of these three principal Chiliasm church fathers: Irenaeus, Justin, or Tertullian. And even then, it must be humbly acknowledged that we could be mistaken.

> "And when the Bridegroom Matthew 25:5, etc. comes, he who has his lamp untrimmed, and not burning with the brightness

of a steady light, is classed among those who obscure the interpretations of the parables, forsaking Him who by His plain announcements freely imparts gifts to all who come to Him, and is excluded from His marriage-chamber."

Tertullian, while mocking certain heretics, reveals that the oil symbolizes holy living—this includes what we can call "financial holiness," based on charity doctrine, which he affirms elsewhere:

"Himself pure from sin, and in all respects holy, He might undergo death on behalf of sinners. Similarly, you who emulate Him in condoning sins, if you yourself have done no sin, plainly suffer in my stead. If, however, you are a sinner, how will the oil of your puny torch be able to suffice for you and for me?"

Methodius of Olympus affirmed the same understanding, explaining that the oil represents holiness and good works:

"So long, then, as this people treasured up nourishment for the light, supplying oil by their works, the light of continence was not extinguished among them, but was ever shining and giving light in the lot of their inheritance. But when the oil failed, by their turning away from the faith to incontinence, the light was entirely extinguished, so that the virgins have again to kindle their lamps by light transmitted from one to another, bringing the light of incorruption to the world from above. Let us then supply now the oil of good works abundantly, and of prudence, being purged from all corruption which would weigh us down; lest, while the Bridegroom tarries, our lamps may also in like manner be extinguished."

While this paper focuses on the Chiliasm fathers, other church fathers also affirmed this interpretation of lamp and oil in Matthew 25 as referring to faith and good works—especially works of charity doctrine. For example, the *Catena Aurea* on Matthew 25 includes the following:

"They that sell are the poor, who, needing the alms of the faithful, made them that recompense which they desire, selling in return for the relief afforded to their wants, a consciousness of good works. This is the abundant fuel of an undying light which may be bought and stored up for the fruits of mercy." – **Hilary of Poitiers (c. 310–c. 367)**

"The 'oil' denotes charity, alms, and every aid rendered to the needy; the lamps denote the gifts of virginity; and He calls them 'foolish,' because after having gone through the greater toil, they lost all for the sake of a less; for it is greater labour to overcome the desires of the flesh than of money." – **John Chrysostom (c. 347–c. 407)**

"And this oil is sold, and at a high cost, nor is it to be got without much toil; so that we understand it not of alms only, but of all virtues and counsels of the teachers." – **Jerome of Stridon (c. 342–c. 420)**

"In the foregoing parable is set forth the condemnation of such as have not prepared sufficient oil for themselves, whether by oil is meant the brightness of good works, or inward joy of conscience, or alms paid in money." – **Gloss from the Catena Aurea, attributed to Thomas Aquinas (c. 1225–c. 1274)**

"But the wise took oil with their lamps, that is, the gladness of good works." – **Augustine of Hippo (c. 354–c. 430)**

"The 'foolish' took lamps, alight indeed at the first, but not supplied with so much oil as should suffice even to the end, being careless respecting the provision of doctrine which comforts faith, and enlightens the lamp of good deeds." – **Origen of Alexandria (c. 185–c. 253)**

Tertullian affirms that the wedding garment—required for those invited to the "marriage of the Lamb," i.e., the first resurrection—is good works. Those without it are cast out:

"He also who shall not be clothed at the marriage feast in the raiment of good works, will have to be bound hand and foot,—as being, of course, raised in his body. So, again, the very reclining at the feast in the kingdom of God, and sitting on Christ's thrones, and standing at last on His right hand and His left, and eating of the tree of life: what are all these but most certain proofs of a bodily appointment and destination?"

Irenaeus likewise declares that the wedding garment represents righteousness, upon which the Holy Spirit rests:

"Still further did He also make it manifest, that we ought, after our calling, to be also adorned with works of righteousness, so that the Spirit of God may rest upon us; for this is the wedding garment... But those who have indeed been called to God's supper, yet have not received the Holy Spirit, because of their

wicked conduct shall be, He declares, cast into outer darkness. …
[T]he same King who gathered from all quarters the faithful to the
marriage of His Son, and who grants them the incorruptible
banquet, [also] orders that man to be cast into outer darkness who
has not on a wedding garment, that is, one who despises it. For as
in the former covenant, with many of them was He not well
pleased (1 Corinthians 10:5), so also is it the case here, that many
are called, but few chosen (Matthew 22:14)."

Tertullian further explains the two-fold meaning of the wedding
garment in Scripture: it represents both holiness of the flesh and the higher
glory reserved for those who make themselves eunuchs for the Kingdom of
Heaven:

"We have also in the Scriptures robes mentioned as
allegorizing the hope of the flesh. Thus in the Revelation of John
it is said: These are they which have not defiled their clothes with
women,—indicating, of course, virgins, and such as have become
eunuchs for the kingdom of heaven's sake (Matthew 19:12).
Therefore they shall be clothed in white raiment (Revelation 3:5),
that is, in the bright beauty of the unwedded flesh. In the gospel
even, the wedding garment may be regarded as the sanctity of the
flesh (Matthew 22:11–12). And so, when Isaiah tells us what sort
of fast the Lord has chosen, and subjoins a statement about the
reward of good works, he says: Then shall your light break forth as
the morning, and your garments shall speedily arise (Isaiah 58:8)...
where he has no thought of cloaks or stuff gowns, but means the
rising of the flesh, which he declared the resurrection of, after its
fall in death. Thus we are furnished even with an allegorical defense
of the resurrection of the body. When, then, we read, Go, my
people, enter into your closets for a little season, until my anger
pass away (Isaiah 26:20), we have in the closets graves, in which
they will have to rest for a little while, who shall have at the end of
the world departed this life in the last furious onset of the power
of Antichrist."

Christ's own words tie the meaning of "lamps burning" directly to
charity doctrine—commanding believers to convert earthly wealth into
heavenly treasure by almsgiving. This doctrine is often neglected by
prosperity gospel teachers, who emphasize the "receiving" part but largely
ignore the command to give sacrificially:

"31But seek the kingdom of God, and all these things shall be added to you. 32Do not fear, little flock, for it is your Father's good pleasure to give you the kingdom. 33Sell what you have and give alms; provide yourselves money bags which do not grow old, a treasure in the heavens that does not fail, where no thief approaches nor moth destroys. 34For where your treasure is, there your heart will be also. 35Let your waist be girded and your lamps burning" (Luke 12:31–35).

The meaning is clear: if one receives earthly wealth and does not use it to build treasure in heaven through acts of charity, then his heart remains fixed on earth, not on heaven. Thus, charity doctrine is one way to keep one's lamp burning, as Christ teaches.

"19Do not lay up for yourselves treasures on earth, where moth and rust destroy and where thieves break in and steal; 20but lay up for yourselves treasures in heaven, where neither moth nor rust destroys and where thieves do not break in and steal. 21For where your treasure is, there your heart will be also" (Matthew 6:19–21).

"21Jesus said to him, 'If you want to be perfect, go, sell what you have and give to the poor, and you will have treasure in heaven; and come, follow Me.' 22But when the young man heard that saying, he went away sorrowful, for he had great possessions" (Matthew 19:21–22).

Finally, Methodius of Olympus once again confirms that good works are necessary to keep our lamps lit, that we may be counted among the five wise virgins:

"Whence sin being dead and destroyed, again I shall rise immortal; and I praise God who by means of death frees His sons from death, and I celebrate lawfully to His honour a festal-day, adorning my tabernacle, that is my flesh, with good works, as there did the five virgins with the five-lighted lamps."

REGARDING SABBATH AND LAW OF MOSES

i) False teachers taught that all Gentile believers must keep the entire Law of Moses:

"1And certain men came down from Judea and taught the brethren, 'Unless you are circumcised according to the custom of

Moses, you cannot be saved.' … 5But some of the sect of the Pharisees who believed rose up, saying, 'It is necessary to circumcise them, and to command them to keep the law of Moses.'"

ii) True teachers taught that Jewish and Gentile believers do not share the same requirements:

> "23To the brethren who are of the Gentiles in Antioch, Syria, and Cilicia: … 24Since we have heard that some who went out from us have troubled you with words, unsettling your souls, saying, 'You must be circumcised and keep the law'—to whom we gave no such commandment— … 28For it seemed good to the Holy Spirit, and to us, to lay upon you no greater burden than these necessary things: 29that you abstain from things offered to idols, from blood, from things strangled, and from sexual immorality. If you keep yourselves from these, you will do well. Farewell."

Note: As clarified below, the other nine commandments are confirmed in various New Testament passages, but these additional instructions emphasize moral portions of the Law of Moses (such as commands against sexual immorality and blood) that are binding on Gentiles as well. These moral commands include prohibitions against same-sex behavior (Leviticus 18:22) and prostitution (Leviticus 19:29), which were not part of the Ten Commandments yet are reiterated as binding here.

Let us now break down the relevant verses:

1. The issue: "You teach all the Jews who are among the Gentiles to forsake Moses" (Acts 21:21).

2. The resolution: "You yourself also walk orderly and keep the law" (Acts 21:24).

3. The interpretation: Jewish Christians may observe non-ceremonial portions of the Torah that are not in conflict with the atoning work of Christ. For instance, Jewish Christians are not permitted to offer animal sacrifices since Christ has fulfilled that requirement.

4. The distinction: Gentile Christians are not held to the same observances as Jewish Christians. As it is written, "But concerning the Gentiles who believe, we have written and decided that they should observe no such thing" (Acts 21:25).

5. The application: Paul, being Jewish, can observe the Sabbath under the principle of Acts 21:24. Fellow Jewish believers may do the same.

6. The clarification: Of the Ten Commandments, nine are restated in the New Testament for Gentile believers. The Sabbath command is not. Instead, Paul explicitly removes Sabbath observance from binding obligation in Colossians 2:16.

Colossians 2:16 plainly teaches that Sabbath-keeping is non-binding for Gentile believers: "Let no one judge you in food or in drink, or regarding a festival or a new moon or sabbaths." If Paul intended for Gentile Christians to observe the Sabbath, he could have simply written, "Keep the Sabbath." Instead, the phrase "let no one judge you" strongly supports the freedom not to observe it. After all, only those who keep the Sabbath feel the need to judge those who do not.

The "rest" discussed in Hebrews 4 is not about weekly Sabbath observance but refers instead to the "seventh day" as a prophetic image of the millennial reign of Christ—a truth affirmed by Irenaeus, who places this fulfillment at Christ's Second Coming and the First Resurrection. He refers to this as "the times of the kingdom," which occur after Christ returns, not before.

Irenaeus further supports this view in his commentary on Colossians 2:16, identifying feast days, fasts, and Sabbaths as displeasing to the Lord when used to judge others and divide the church. He does not use Colossians 2:16 to mandate Sabbath-keeping for Gentiles.

Tertullian, arguing against Marcion, also affirms that Colossians 2:16 teaches the Sabbath has been abolished in its ceremonial form for Gentile believers. He explains that the passage transitions us from the shadows (Sabbaths, feast days) to the substance (Christ).

Christ did not say that His disciples did not break Sabbath regulations but rather declared that His disciples were guiltless despite breaking them. Irenaeus explains that Christians are spiritual priests, and just as Old Testament priests could profane the Sabbath without guilt, so too are Christians not judged for Sabbath violations.

The Protestant Reformers did not teach that the Sunday Lord's Day replaced the Sabbath. Calvin even cautioned that attributing the same sanctity to Sunday as the Sabbath led to superstition. He emphasized the moral principle of resting one day in seven, without legislating a specific day. The Westminster divines similarly spoke of Sunday as a day for worship, charity, and works of necessity and mercy. Augustine likewise acknowledged that the Sabbath was the only commandment in the Decalogue not binding on Christians.

The earliest Christians gathered on Sunday not as a law but as a voluntary memorial of Christ. Their gatherings included acts of charity and mutual sharing, not legalistic observances.

> "Now all who believed were together, and had all things in common, and sold their possessions and goods, and divided them among all, as anyone had need" (Acts 2:44–45).

"And let us consider one another in order to stir up love and good works, not forsaking the assembling of ourselves together ..." (Hebrews 10:24–25).

This practice supports the idea that if believers cannot give away their possessions during life, they may donate them at death, fulfilling charity doctrine through their will. The giving is measured relatively, and the focus remains on voluntary generosity rather than Sabbath observance.

Irenaeus teaches that the Mosaic Sabbath was only given to Israel. The true fulfillment of the Sabbath for Christians is spiritual—serving God daily, being free from covetousness, and preparing for the millennial kingdom.

> "For we have been counted, says the Apostle Paul, all the day long as sheep for the slaughter ... consecrated to God, and ministering continually to our faith, and persevering in it, and abstaining from all avarice ... the man who shall have persevered in serving God shall, in a state of rest, partake of God's table."

He further points out that men like Abraham, Lot, Noah, and Enoch were righteous and justified without ever keeping the Sabbath or being circumcised. This shows that the Sabbath was not a law by nature, and the covenant at Horeb was made not with the patriarchs, but only later with Israel (Deuteronomy 5:2).

Tertullian affirms the same truth, citing the righteousness of Abel, Noah, Enoch, and Melchizedek—all uncircumcised and inobservant of the Sabbath—yet pleasing to God.

Justin Martyr agrees, stating that Sabbaths and circumcision were given because of Israel's disobedience and were not binding on Christians.

Thus, the apostolic verdict of Colossians 2:16 remains: "So let no one judge you in food or in drink, or regarding a festival or a new moon or sabbaths."

Galatians 3:26–29 is sometimes misused to erase all distinctions between Jew and Gentile, male and female, or slave and free. But this passage refers to the spiritual equality of all believers in inheritance—not to temporal roles or church order. The Abrahamic promise is realized in the millennial kingdom, not now through prosperity.

The same Paul who wrote Galatians 3 also gave detailed gender roles for the church. He forbade women from teaching or exercising authority over men. He instructed that women should remain silent in churches regarding theological discussion, directing them instead to learn from their husbands at home. These commands are not culturally relative but are grounded in creation order and spiritual authority.

> "For the husband is head of the wife, as also Christ is head of the church" (Ephesians 5:23).

> "Let your women keep silent in the churches, for they are not permitted to speak" (1 Corinthians 14:34).

God's Word stands above all human culture: "Making the word of God of no effect through your tradition" (Mark 7:13).

Even the slave imagery in Galatians 3 points to future reward: "Knowing that from the Lord you will receive the reward of the inheritance" (Colossians 3:24). God does not endorse slavery, but He does promise eternal reward for those who suffer unjustly in obedience.

"Behold, to obey is better than sacrifice" (1 Samuel 15:22).

The claim that we must keep the Sabbath because Christ did is a flawed argument. Christ also kept all 613 laws. If Christians are bound to all that Christ did, we would also need to be circumcised and offer sacrifices—yet the Bible forbids both for Gentile believers (Galatians 5:2–4).

Thus, the "good works" required by Chiliasm church fathers do not include Sabbath-keeping for Gentile believers.

CHILIASM CHURCH FATHERS DID NOT TEACH TITHING

Irenaeus of Lyons writes that the Lord did not bring up the **tithe command** toward **Gentile believers** under the **New Testament**. In the quote that follows, Irenaeus clearly shows that while some laws were extended—such as **giving to enemies** without regard for their evil intentions in order to emulate God the Father—**no compulsory giving** was commanded. Thus, **no replacement form of tithing** was introduced either, since if tithing were a command, it would have to be **mandatory**. Notably,

Irenaeus testifies that **tithing was not commanded**; instead, **charity doctrine**—sharing all our possessions with the poor—was taught, not only toward **neighbors** but even toward **enemies**. He stresses that the extent to which one obeys this determines one's **gradation in the Kingdom**, and that those who do not obey or give hypocritically do not possess the **love of God**:

> "And instead of the law enjoining the giving of tithes, [He told us] to **share** (Matthew 19:21) all our possessions with the poor; and **not to love our neighbours only**, but even **our enemies**; and not merely to be liberal givers and bestowers, but even that we should **present a gratuitous gift to those who take away our goods**… so that you may not follow him as a slave, but may as a free man go before him, showing yourself in all things kindly disposed and useful to your neighbour, **not regarding their evil intentions**, but performing your kind offices, **assimilating yourself to the Father**, who makes His sun to rise upon the evil and the good, and sends rain upon the just and unjust" (Matthew 5:45).

Irenaeus emphasizes that the true spirit of giving includes **not worrying about how others might misuse our generosity**, but instead **trusting God** and obeying the **spirit of grace**. Thus, whether we give our **time**, **possessions**, or **money**, it must not be limited to a local church alone but extended toward the **community at large**, in line with **Christ's commands**.

Though **Justin of Rome** does not have a surviving quote directly referencing tithing, he clearly taught that **no compulsion in giving** existed—implying the **absence of any tithing doctrine**. This aligns with Irenaeus and Tertullian. Justin writes:

> "And the wealthy among us **help the needy**… and there is a distribution to each, and a participation of that over which thanks have been given, and to those who are absent a portion is sent by the deacons. And they who are **well to do, and willing**, give what **each thinks fit**; and what is collected is deposited with the president, who **succours the orphans and widows** and those who, through sickness or any other cause, are in want, and those who are in bonds and the strangers sojourning among us, and in a word takes care of **all who are in need**."

Tertullian also affirms that the early church was built upon the **doctrine of charity**. The church collected funds **willingly**, and **no tithes** or any **obligatory giving** is mentioned. Importantly, there was no place for

prosperity gospel practices—no **buying or selling of the gospel**, nor **luxurious lifestyles** funded by church donations. He explains:

> "The tried men of our elders preside over us, obtaining that honour not by purchase, but by established character. There is **no buying and selling** of any sort in the things of God. Though we have our **treasure chest**, it is not made up of **purchase-money**, as of a religion that has its price. On the monthly day, if he likes, each puts in a small donation; but only **if it be his pleasure**, and only if he be able: for there is **no compulsion; all is voluntary.** These gifts are, as it were, **piety's deposit fund.** For they are not taken thence and spent on **feasts, and drinking-bouts, and eating-houses**, but to **support and bury poor people**, to **supply the wants of boys and girls destitute of means and parents,** and of **old persons confined now to the house**; such, too, as have suffered **shipwreck**; and if there happen to be any in the **mines**, or **banished to the islands**, or **shut up in the prisons**, for nothing but their fidelity to the cause of God's Church, they become the **nurslings of their confession.** But it is mainly the deeds of a **love so noble** that lead many to put a brand upon us."

Tertullian also notes that **charity**—not tithing—is the commanded act that reflects the **love of God** and results in **cleansing**:

> "Same God belongs the **cleansing of a man's external and internal nature**, both alike being in the power of Him who prefers **mercy** not only to man's washing, but even to **sacrifice.** For He subjoins the command: **Give what you possess as alms, and all things shall be clean unto you** (Luke 11:41)… In like manner, He upbraids them for **tithing paltry herbs**, but at the same time **passing over hospitality and the love of God** (Luke 11:42). The whole point of the rebuke lay in this, that they cared about **small matters** in His service—of course, to whom they failed to exhibit their **weightier duties** when He commanded them."

Therefore, the **"good works"** · required by the **Chiliasm church fathers** never included the **tithing doctrine** for Christians. Instead, they emphasized **charity doctrine** coupled with **holiness** to prepare as one of the **5 wise virgins**, which makes the Christian walk **perfect.**

CONCLUSION

It is worth noting that the father of the Reformation, **Martin Luther**, did **not believe in Sabbath-keeping** or **tithing** as part of **good works** either. He wrote:

> "**Tithing**: But the other commandments of Moses, which are not [implanted in all men] by nature, the Gentiles do not hold. Nor do these pertain to the Gentiles, such as the **tithe** and others equally fine which I wish we had too. …
>
> **Sabbath**: Again one can prove it from the third commandment that Moses does not pertain to Gentiles and Christians."

The **Augsburg Confession** echoes this same position:

> "**Colossians 2:16**: Let no man, therefore, judge you in meat, or in drink, or in respect of a holy-day, or of the **Sabbath-day**; … as of **matrimony** or of **tithes**, etc., they have it by **human right** … For those who judge that by the authority of the Church the observance of the **Lord's Day** instead of the **Sabbath-day** was ordained as a thing **necessary**, do greatly err … example of **Christian liberty**, and might know that the keeping neither of the **Sabbath** nor of any other day is **necessary**."

It is important to observe that when the **Augsburg Confession** was written, **tithes were not collected by individual pastors**, but rather by the **government**, which only shared a small portion with the Church. This meant that tithes were used for **secular spending**, not exclusively for **religious purposes**, in direct contrast to modern practice.

By **God's grace**, we are called to strive to be among the **five wise virgins**, not the **five foolish virgins**. This is accomplished by **understanding and obeying** what the **giants of the faith** have taught—especially the **Chiliasm church fathers** and **Protestant Reformers**—who consistently upheld **holiness through abstinence from sin**, and emphasized **charity doctrine** as the **primary good work** that puts **love into action**. In this way, the **Holy Spirit of God** abides in us, and we walk in the manner that leads to being part of the **elect salvation**, prepared to enter the **wedding of the Lamb**.

CHAPTER 8 Did Christ Imply Non-Elect Salvation in Matthew 19:16–22?

CHRISTIAN SALVATION IN MATTHEW 19:16–22

Here is a scholarly translation of the passage:

> "Now behold, one came and said to Him, 'Good Teacher, what good thing shall I do that I may have eternal life?'
> So He said to him, 'Why do you call Me good? No one is good but One, that is, God. But if you want to enter into life, keep the commandments.'
> He said to Him, 'Which ones?'
> Jesus said, 'You shall not murder,' 'You shall not commit adultery,' 'You shall not steal,' 'You shall not bear false witness,' 'Honor your father and your mother,' and, 'You shall love your neighbor as yourself.'
> The young man said to Him, 'All these things I have kept from my youth. What do I still lack?'
> Jesus said to him, 'If you want to be perfect, go, sell what you have and give to the poor, and you will have treasure in heaven; and come, follow Me.'
> But when the young man heard that saying, he went away sorrowful, for he had great possessions." (Matthew 19:16–22)

A proper way to understand these verses is to analyze them in light of the summary Christ Himself gives in the later portion of this chapter. That context helps distinguish between what is essential for **eternal life** and what pertains to **heavenly reward**. The consistent theme affirmed across Christianity is that there are **requirements for entering the kingdom**, which include **repentance from sin**, a principle clearly implied in this interaction with the rich young man.

Christ first presents **commandment-keeping** as the initial path to **enter into life**. This rich man claims to have obeyed these commands from his youth. However, Christ then challenges him with the higher standard of **perfection**, commanding him to **sell all he has and give to the poor,** promising in return "treasure in heaven." It is critical to note here that Christ only quoted **commandments that relate to one's obligations toward fellow man**, not the full Decalogue. This omission is not accidental, as it draws attention to this man's **lack of generosity and love**, which itself reveals **financial idolatry** and thus hidden sin.

The phrase **"if you want to be perfect"** serves as a dividing line between two classes: those who enter life by basic obedience and those who attain the higher standard of **perfection**, evidenced by radical self-sacrifice. In Matthew 19:28, Christ connects this perfection to the **resurrection** and **reign** of the saints, promising rulership to those who follow Him fully. This proves that **eternal life** is distinct from **heavenly rewards** such as "treasure in heaven" and reigning with Christ in His kingdom.

Therefore, the passage introduces the possibility that some may receive **eternal life** without becoming part of the **bride** or elect class—those who rule with Christ. In this light, **non-elect salvation** becomes a valid theological consideration. It refers to those who are not part of the **first resurrection** or **marriage supper of the Lamb**, yet are granted life by the **grace of Christ's ransom**. This distinction is reinforced in Matthew 19 by the way Christ separates those who simply **enter life** from those who **attain treasure in heaven**.

Many modern Christians advocate for **absolute assurance**, asserting that all who believe in Christ will obtain **eternal life**, even if they fall into sin, and that their only loss will be of **rewards**, not life itself. However, this view is not without dispute. John MacArthur, for example, confronts this doctrine by citing John 6:66 and Judas Iscariot as warnings that **not all who start in the faith persevere**. He implies that **mere profession** is not the same as genuine conversion.

Calvinists similarly warn against **cultural Christianity**, where a person claims faith but lives in sin, denying Christ in conduct. Even **regular churchgoers**, they argue, may be **unsaved** if they do not **endure in sanctification**. Inserra states plainly: "Self-proclaimed Christians who worship a god that requires no self-sacrifice, no obedience, no submission, and no surrender are not worshiping the God of the Bible, no matter how much they claim they love Jesus." This warning is consistent with the message of Matthew 19:16–22.

Thus, Christ's conversation with the rich young ruler does not simply expose this man's heart, but also implicitly reveals **tiers within salvation**. The first tier is **entry into life** through obedience to God's moral commands and faith in Christ. The second is **perfection**, characterized by sacrificial charity and total surrender. The former may represent **non-elect salvation**, while the latter reveals the **elect bride of Christ**.

FINANCIAL HOLINESS AS CHRISTIAN PERFECTION IN MATTHEW 19:16–22

We find Christ issuing a startling call to **perfection** through a **financial command**—to give to the poor. This invitation was addressed to a rich man who had generally kept the **Torah's major commandments**, yet was still **"lacking"** (Matthew 19:20). While the requirement for perfection in this case was financial, the **commands of Christ** toward perfection extend into many other areas of life. These broader principles are chiefly laid out in the **Beatitudes** found in the **Sermon on the Mount** (Matthew 5–7).

Christians have long struggled to interpret what this **perfection** means. Some have interpreted it merely as "achieving the purpose for which they are intended to live," which varies by person. However, such an individualistic view often misses the universal moral standards Christ emphasized. Secular philosophies and Jewish traditions have attempted to define or interpret this concept, but such sources must be approached with extreme caution. Frequently, Christ explicitly corrected **Jewish misconceptions**, particularly evident in His formulaic rebukes: **"You have heard it said... but I say to you"** (cf. Matthew 5:21–22, 27–28, 33–34, etc.).

In the matter of **money**, Korver rightly notes that in Matthew 19:21 Christ was referring to **"treasure in heaven"**, not **entrance into heaven**. However, such a distinction can become dangerous if used to justify **ignoring the poor**, since **financial negligence** can also lead to condemnation. The doctrine of **financial holiness**—that is, living with **monetary righteousness**—is not merely a **higher reward category**, but is tied directly to **salvific obedience** when the love of God must be manifested in material terms. Church fathers and Reformers confirm this strongly.

The parable of the **rich man and Lazarus** (Luke 16:19–31) is a key passage where **financial sin** is shown to result in **hellfire**. Some modern Jewish interpretations attempt to downplay or allegorize it, but early Christian thinkers viewed this as a **historical account** and not merely symbolic.

Irenaeus of Lyons (c. 130–202) affirms that the rich man was condemned to **Hades** for being **unmerciful to poor Lazarus**. This mirrors the warning of **James the Apostle**, who declares that the **hoarding of wealth** without helping the poor will "eat your flesh like fire" (James 5:3), indicating a clear connection between **luxurious living** and final judgment. Irenaeus echoes this same theme.

Tertullian (c. 155–220) refutes the claim that this story is merely allegorical by reasoning that **even parables must be rooted in real-life elements**, and Christ's mention of **Abraham** proves the reality of this narrative. Christ would not issue such warnings **if the danger were not real**. Tertullian further asserts that **bishops** who ignore the poor and fail to **exercise hospitality**—as required by **"Moses and the prophets"**—may likewise end in **hellfire**.

Martin Luther (1483–1546) explains that it is not enough to **"depart from evil"**; one must also **"do good"**. **John Calvin (1509–1564)** is even more explicit, stating that the rich man in Luke 16 went to hell **"for refusing to raise a finger to help the poor man."**

Why did Christ connect **perfection** with **financial renunciation?** Those who give up **all** cannot be guilty of **withholding from the poor**, because they **retain nothing** for themselves. They survive on the barest **necessities**, eliminating any chance of **greed**. God's standard of perfection defines it as **sin** even when one simply **fails to do good** in areas where they are able (cf. James 4:17), and this clearly includes the **financial context**. One is already sinning if one **refuses to give** when in a position to do so.

This is a key reason why the **first New Testament church** held all possessions **in common** (Acts 2:44–45; Acts 4:32–35). Although this level of unity is impractical today due to economic and social complexities, the principle remains: we must **give by relative measure**, according to ability.

True **unity** in the Church is **incomplete** without this financial aspect. **Loving others as oneself** is fulfilled only when one spends **equally** on others and on self, as far as one is able. In contrast, many professing Christians spend **excessively** on personal pleasures, giving **little** to others— even while **appearing holy outwardly**. But love for God is proven through the **sharing of spiritual and physical goods** (1 John 3:17), and without such **charity**, one's salvation may be called into question. The story of the rich man and Lazarus makes this painfully clear.

Unbelievers often **mock Christian generosity**, especially when it extends to **strangers, unbelievers, or even enemies**. But **Christ commands** exactly that (Luke 6:35). **John Chrysostom (c. 347–407)** taught that **charity** is a **higher virtue than virginity**, correcting those who prioritized **fasting and prayer** over **almsgiving**. Chrysostom ranks **almsgiving** as the **core of perfection**, in agreement with Christ in Matthew 19:21. The **prophets** likewise affirm this, such as **Isaiah**, who links good works—especially to the poor—with true righteousness (Isaiah 58:6–11).

Charitable giving is one of the **gifts of grace** (Romans 12:8). It is uniquely praised in Scripture when done **"beyond one's ability"** (2 Corinthians 8:3), especially by those who are themselves **poor**. Because clean financial gain requires **hard work**, giving it away amounts to a kind of **life sacrifice**, modeled on Christ Himself. In this way, **giving to the poor** is likened to **laying down one's life**, thus participating in Christ's example, even within the domain of **money**.

NON-ELECT SALVATION POSSIBILITY WITH MATTHEW 19:16–22

Koplitz observes that in the **Greek educational model**, the instructor is always assumed to be correct—a method that has heavily influenced Biblical institutions and churches today. By contrast, the **Hebraic method of instruction** encourages the student to **challenge what is heard**, leading to a deeper understanding and eventually enabling the student to become a teacher as well. This dynamic is evident in **Christ's interaction** with the rich young ruler in **Matthew 19:16–22**. Rather than immediately listing a set of rules when asked, "What good thing shall I do that I may have eternal life?", Christ first responds with a **counter-question**, prompting introspection. Only after engaging the young man's understanding does Christ affirm certain commandments and expand on what he lacked.

Several observations may be made from this exchange:

First, Christ did **not** require the man to keep **all 613 commandments** of the Torah to inherit eternal life.

Second, when asked "Which commandments?", Christ quotes **only the last six** of the **Ten Commandments**, all of which concern **human-to-human relationships**. He **omits** the first four commandments, which focus on a person's **relationship with God**. This distinction raises the possibility that Christ might be **opening the door to non-elect salvation**—that is, salvation for those who do **not** fully know or worship God, but **keep the moral laws** relating to other humans. If someone keeps the first four commandments, they would be aligned with **elect salvation**, since those deal with direct **obedience to God**. However, even the **fourth commandment**, the Sabbath, is not imposed on **Gentile believers**, as confirmed by both **earliest church fathers** and **Protestant Reformers**. **Irenaeus** interpreted the Sabbath **spiritually**, seeing its observance as a call to **abstain from avarice** and avoid hoarding wealth: "Sabbaths taught that we should continue day by day in God's service… abstaining from all avarice, and not acquiring or possessing treasures upon earth."

Third, Christ includes the command to **"love your neighbor as yourself"**, which is not one of the Ten Commandments but is taken from **Leviticus 19:18**. Christ expands this command to an **"enemies-level"** in the parable of the **Good Samaritan** (Luke 10:25–37), showing that **love must extend beyond cultural and religious boundaries**.

Fourth, the rich man claimed to have kept all these commandments. In response, Christ said he still lacked something and instructed him to **sell all he had** and **give to the poor**, then to **follow Him**. This addition of **charity doctrine** and **discipleship** goes beyond the moral commandments and appears to form the **complete picture of elect salvation**—righteous behavior plus **active obedience** to Christ Himself.

Fifth, the **parable of the Good Samaritan** may support the idea of **non-elect salvation**. Christ said that Samaritans **"do not know God"** (cf. John 4:22), yet the Samaritan in the parable practiced **compassion** toward his **enemy**, the Jew. This could represent a **non-Christian** doing **charity doctrine** to Christians—mirroring the **surprised sheep** of the nations in Matthew 25:31–40 who are unaware of serving Christ, asking, "When did we see you hungry…?" Yet Christ identifies them as **"righteous"** based on their works toward **His brethren**, implying these are **non-elects** (not disciples) saved based on **charity toward Christians**.

Sixth, if this interpretation is valid, then such individuals are **not saved by works**, but by being **granted belief after seeing**. This is echoed in **John 6:29, 36, 40**, where Christ rebukes those who **saw Him but did not believe**. The implication is that **seeing Him and believing** could still lead to salvation—similar to **Thomas**, who only believed after seeing the risen Lord. Such individuals might correspond to those in **1 Corinthians 3:15**, who are **"saved, yet so as by fire."** They differ from the **rewarded** Christians of **1 Corinthians 3:14**, whose **living faith** produces **at least thirtyfold works** (cf. Matthew 13:8).

Seventh, Christ stated that **prophets continued until John the Baptist** (Matthew 11:13), not merely until **Malachi**. This may leave room for the **Deuterocanonical books** such as **Wisdom of Solomon** and **2 Esdras**, which occur between Malachi and John. Although **not canonical**, some of these writings offer **early views** of afterlife and judgment. For example, **2 Maccabees 12:42–45** promotes **prayers for the dead**, paired with a **charitable sin offering**—not prayers to the dead, which are unbiblical.

> "He made a reconciliation for the dead, that they might be delivered from sin."

This suggests a primitive **purgatorial concept**, though not required for the non-elect salvation view presented here. The point remains: **Christ celebrated Hanukkah**, a festival originating from the **Maccabees** (John 10:22–23). If the Maccabees were **false prophets**, why would Christ participate in a feast associated with them? The fact that **Christ does not correct** the Jewish practice of prayers for the dead, though not endorsing it either, leaves room for **speculative reflection**, always **submitted to Sola Scriptura**.

Eighth, additional early **Orthodox and Catholic writings** (excluding heretical sources) contain statements that seem to support the **non-elect salvation possibility**, especially when aligned with **Chiliasm prophetic timelines**.

i) In the **first resurrection, Irenaeus** and **Lactantius** affirm that all **Christians and righteous saints** of the past rise to reign with Christ at His **public second coming**, which ends the reign of the antichrist and inaugurates the **Millennial Kingdom**.

ii) In the **second resurrection, Lactantius** teaches that all remaining individuals rise for **judgment and condemnation**, with **no hope** remaining.

> "At the same time shall take place that second and public resurrection of all, in which the unrighteous shall be raised to everlasting punishments…"

Yet **Irenaeus** quotes the **Matthew 25 sheep and goats passage** and attributes it to the **entire human race**. This suggests that some who are **not part of the first resurrection**—those raised **after the thousand years**—may still be saved. Since **first and second resurrections** are separated by **a millennium**, the sheep in Matthew 25:34 could represent **non-elect righteous** saved during the **second resurrection** based on **charity doctrine** alone.

The Jewish doctrine of **righteous Gentiles** keeping the **Seven Noahide Laws** may be a shadow of this idea. However, in light of **Matthew 19**, the standard appears higher: the **last six commandments** of the Decalogue. Missing among both Noahide and the Matthew 19 list is the command **not to worship idols**, which is tied to the **first two commandments**. If a person **abstains from idolatry**, that would potentially make them **elect**, not non-elect.

In conclusion, Christ's encounter with the rich man in **Matthew 19:16–22**, along with other Scriptural and historical references, offers serious biblical grounds for the **possibility of non-elect salvation—not by earning it through works**, but by demonstrating a **righteous nature** consistent with the **moral law**, particularly through **charity** toward Christ's people. Such individuals may be **saved after death, upon seeing Christ**, and **repenting**, distinct from those **saved with reward** in this life.

CONCLUSION

The **non-elect salvation possibility** may pertain specifically to **righteous Gentiles** who, during their earthly lives, fulfilled the **last six of the Ten Commandments**, those pertaining to **human relationships**. If this interpretation holds true, then in **Matthew 19:16–22**, Christ—in His **foreknowledge**—may be illustrating why the **rich man**, who failed to fulfill even those six commands in the financial context toward others, **might still be saved**, but only into a **non-elect category of salvation**.

This could explain why **Christ omits the first four commandments**, those dealing directly with God, when responding to the rich man. According to **Mark 12:29–31**, fulfilling the **greatest commandment**—to love God—**requires** loving one's neighbor as oneself. This implies that without **obedience to the human-centered commands**, one cannot truly love God, as the two are **interdependent**.

The keeping of these six commandments is plausible for non-elect individuals because these commands relate to **human conduct**, and even **imperfect Christians** strive for them. When such **righteousness** is found in unbelievers, it is still by the **grace of God**, not by human merit, and may signify those **marked out** for this lower-tier salvation. Apart from the **surprised sheep of the nations in Matthew 25:31–46**, the case of **Cyrus the Great** is instructive: God used Cyrus to enact the **charity doctrine** of freeing the Jews, despite Cyrus **never knowing God** before or after this act (Isaiah 45:4-5). Similarly, **Cornelius** was accepted by God for his **charity and prayers** even **before conversion** (Acts 10:1–4). That he later **believed in Christ** through a divine encounter shows he transitioned into **elect salvation**, illustrating both categories at work in a single life.

We must approach **prophetic interpretation** with caution, in reverence for the warning of **Revelation 22:18–19**, which solemnly declares:

> "For I testify to everyone who hears the words of the prophecy of this book: If anyone adds to these things, God will

add to him the plagues… and if anyone takes away… God shall take away his part from the Book of Life…"

In view of this, the **non-elect salvation idea** is presented **not** as a new doctrine, but as a **scholarly, Scripturally-based hypothesis**, acknowledging that **the Holy Spirit** did **not** reveal this interpretation directly. This restraint helps avoid the spiritual danger of **adding to or subtracting from Scripture**.

That said, **Revelation 22:17** may contain a subtle reference to this idea. It reads:

> "And the Spirit and the bride say, 'Come!' And let him who hears say, 'Come!' And let him who thirsts come. Whoever desires, let him take the water of life freely."

This final invitation, voiced by **the bride (the Church)**, appears to be directed **not to herself**, but to **outsiders**—those who are **not yet part of the elect**. It's notable that partaking of the **water of life** implies entry into the **final sinless resurrection state**, and yet **those partaking here** also need **healing** from the **leaves of the Tree of Life** (Revelation 22:2). This takes place **after** the **Great White Throne Judgment** (Revelation 20:11–15), in the **New Heavens and Earth**, where **the Book of Life** has already been revealed (Revelation 21:27).

According to the **chiliasm timeline** of **Lactantius** and especially **Irenaeus, Christians** had already **partaken of the water of life 1,000 years earlier**, during the **First Resurrection** (Revelation 20:4–6). Therefore, it is difficult to envision a scenario in which **Christians** still require healing **after** a full millennium of glorified resurrection life. This suggests that the ones needing healing in Revelation 22:2 may belong to **a different group**—the **saved nations** (Revelation 21:24–26), distinct from the **bride**.

These nations, over whom **the kings of the earth** rule (Revelation 21:24), could consist of **non-elect saved individuals**, whereas Christians appear to be in **heavenly glory** at this point (Revelation 21:9), reigning as **kings and priests** (Revelation 1:6). This distinction reinforces the concept that **different classes of salvation** may exist in the eternal state, according to one's **response to truth** in this life or possibly in the **spirit world**.

In sum, even if this view of **non-elect salvation** proves incorrect, its presentation here is **guarded, non-dogmatic**, and always subject to the **authority of Holy Scripture alone**. The heart of this essay is to examine the possibility **honestly**, not presumptuously. By not claiming divine revelation, we avoid violating the sacred warnings of Revelation. We have merely posed the idea as a **Biblical possibility** in harmony with **Matthew 19:16–22**, supported by **prophetic sequencing**, and consistent with the writings of select **Chiliasm Church Fathers** and **Scriptural principles of divine justice**.

CHAPTER 9 Other Church Fathers or Quotes for Non-Election Salvation

Any Church Father quote suggesting someone being saved in the **Spirit World**, whether in **Hades** or even from the **Lake of Fire**, may be a possible reference to **Non-Elect Salvation**. We uphold the classical Protestant belief that **Elect Salvation** does not undergo any Spirit World judgment, as seen in Scriptures such as:

i) Elect Salvation does not undergo any Hades judgment:

"Most assuredly, I say to you, he who hears My word and believes in Him who sent Me has everlasting life, and shall not come into judgment, but has passed from death into life."

ii) Elect Salvation does not undergo any Lake of Fire judgment:

"He who has an ear, let him hear what the Spirit says to the churches. He who overcomes shall not be hurt by the second death."

"Blessed and holy is he who has part in the first resurrection. Over such the second death has no power, but they shall be priests of God and of Christ, and shall reign with Him a thousand years."

1. Book of 1 Enoch

In the Book of 1 Enoch (recognized as canonical only by the Ethiopian Orthodox Church), chapter 50 describes a scene that aligns with the **Chiliasm Prophecy**: a transformation occurs among the **elect**, who are described as no longer being flesh and blood but as clothed in "the light of days," "glory," and "honour." This transformation occurs on Judgment Day (verse 2), implying the **Second Resurrection** context. The elect are victorious, and the unrighteous are allowed to witness their glory so that they might repent.

But those who repent at this stage are described as having "no honour" (verse 3). This implies they are not elect. Nevertheless, it says they "shall be saved" through the name of the Lord, and that "the Lord of Spirits will have compassion on them." This suggests a **Non-Elect Salvation** possibility distinct from the reward and glory of the elect. The final verses declare eternal condemnation for those who do not repent, after which divine mercy ceases.

> "1 And in those days a change shall take place for the holy and elect,
> And the light of days shall abide upon them,
> 2 On the day of affliction on which evil shall have been treasured up against the sinners.
> And the righteous shall be victorious in the name of the Lord of Spirits:
> And He will cause the others to witness (this)
> That they may repent
> And forgo the works of their hands.
> 3 They shall have no honour through the name of the Lord of Spirits,
> Yet through His name shall they be saved,
> And the Lord of Spirits will have compassion on them, for His compassion is great.
> 4 And He is righteous also in His judgment,
> And in the presence of His glory unrighteousness also shall not maintain itself:
> At His judgment the unrepentant shall perish before Him.
> 5 And from henceforth I will have no mercy on them, saith the Lord of Spirits."

2. Shepherd of Hermas

Tertullian expressed discomfort with the **Shepherd of Hermas** because it appears to teach a **Non-Elect Salvation** possibility, particularly for certain sinners such as adulterers. Nonetheless, he admits its authority, saying:

"But I would yield my ground to you, if the Scripture of the Shepherd, which is the only one which favours adulterers, had deserved to find a place in the Divine canon; if it had not been habitually judged by every council of Churches (even of your own) among apocryphal and false (writings); … I, however, imbibe the Scriptures of that Shepherd who cannot be broken."

Even though Tertullian had reservations, he still respected the text as containing unbreakable truth. This method of critical but honest examination is the same approach taken here in this essay.

The **Shepherd of Hermas** (also called "The Pastor") was considered **Scripture** by several early Church Fathers, including **St. Irenaeus of Lyons** and even **Tertullian**. It appeared in early biblical collections such as the **Roman/Muratorian Canon** and the **Codex Sinaiticus**.

Irenaeus quotes the Shepherd of Hermas as Scripture, writing:

"Truly, then, the Scripture declared, which says, 'First of all believe that there is one God, who has established all things, and completed them, and having caused that from what had no being, all things should come into existence: He who contains all things, and is Himself contained by no one.'"

This exact phrase matches what is preserved in the Shepherd of Hermas today.

The **Muratorian Canon** (c. 170 C.E.) affirms the text's authority:

"But Hermas wrote The Shepherd very recently, in our times, in the city of Rome, while bishop Pius, his brother, was occupying the chair of the church of the city of Rome. And therefore, it ought indeed to be read; but it cannot be read publicly to the people in church either among the Prophets, whose number is complete, or among the Apostles, for it is after their time."

St. Athanasius the Great did not include it in his canon of 27 books, but he placed the Shepherd on the same level as the Book of Esther, which Protestants accept as Scripture today. That parallel opens the possibility that the Shepherd of Hermas may still hold weight, especially in understanding early Christian beliefs on postmortem salvation.

The Shepherd describes **Elect Salvation** as entering into the "Tower of Repentance," which represents the **Church**. The angel in the vision says:

"Many indeed shall hear, and hearing, some shall be glad, and some shall weep. But even these, if they hear and repent, shall also rejoice. Hear, then, the parables of the tower; … The tower which you see building is myself, the Church, who have appeared to you now and on the former occasion."

St. Irenaeus also makes use of this concept, writing:

"… the beautiful elect tower being also raised everywhere. For the illustrious Church is [now] everywhere, and everywhere is the winepress dug: because those who do receive the Spirit are everywhere."

Yet, Hermas introduces a **Non-Elect Salvation** path for those who are rejected stones, meaning people who were once receptive to the Gospel but ultimately failed to live in holiness. These are not allowed into the Tower but are promised a place in a much more inferior region after they have suffered punishment for their sins. The angelic messenger explains:

"Do you wish to know who are the others which fell near the waters, but could not be rolled into them? These are they who have heard the word and wish to be baptized in the name of the Lord; but when the chastity demanded by the truth comes into their recollection, they draw back, and again walk after their own wicked desires... Is repentance possible for all those stones which have been cast away and did not fit into the building of the tower...? Repentance, said she, is yet possible, but in this tower, they cannot find a suitable place. But in another and much inferior place they will be laid, and that, too, only when they have been tortured and completed the days of their sins. And on this account will they be transferred, because they have partaken of the righteous Word. And then only will they be removed from their punishments when the thought of repenting of the evil deeds which they have done has come into their hearts. But if it does not come into their hearts, they will not be saved on account of the hardness of their heart."

In this vision, the *Elect* are identified with the **Church**, but another category of people receives mercy after judgment and torture. They are not elect and cannot enter the tower, but they are shown mercy elsewhere. This fits the idea of **Non-Elect Salvation**—not an eternal damnation, yet not the full reward of the elect.

According to this text, such individuals can only be saved if they **repent** after their punishment and have previously *partaken of the righteous Word*. This possibly refers to their earlier reception of Christ's teachings, especially **holiness** and **charity doctrine** commandments. Though they rejected obedience at the time, the Shepherd implies that posthumous repentance may still lead to a form of salvation—though clearly inferior.

We can match the **"elect tower salvation"** as referring to the **final new heavens** abode, while the **non-elect salvation outside the tower** pertains to the **final new earth** abode, based on our earlier discussions. Also, take careful note: if the Roman Catholic doctrine of purgatory were correct, then these souls would be placed back **into the tower** after their purgatorial cleansing. That, however, is not what is being taught here. The salvation of these individuals is explicitly said to be **outside the tower** (i.e., not within the Church), which rules out the Roman Catholic claim and instead implies a distinct **non-elect salvation possibility**. Observe also that these individuals are **not described as repenting on earth**, despite having **heard the Gospel**, because they **walked back into their own evil desires**. This makes it clear that they are not part of the unlearned or unreached, nor can they be equated with those who never had the opportunity to respond. Their opportunity came, and they rejected it during their earthly life.

3. St. Ambrose (c. 340–397 C.E.), Archbishop of Milan

St. Ambrose's words offer an early glimpse into a potential **non-elect salvation** scenario by suggesting that **even those not granted the elect reward** may still obtain a form of mercy **after death**, albeit without the honor associated with the first resurrection. His statement acknowledges that **some souls may be in a condition where they are not altogether cast away**, but neither are they among the blessed who reign with Christ.

He writes:

> "So also God, who prefers mercy to sacrifice, does not reserve His mercy for the time of reward only, but exercises it even at the time of punishment. He consoles the penitent in hell, and brings relief to those who are tormented by the chastisements of judgment."

This comment does not support universal salvation. It clearly maintains the **justice of divine chastisement** while simultaneously asserting that God's mercy **can extend into judgment itself**, offering consolation to those being punished. If that mercy results in some measure of restoration or preservation, then this may align with a **non-elect salvation**, where the souls are **not annihilated**, nor are they rewarded with ruling as kings and priests, but rather **granted survival or healing outside the tower**—much like those **healed by the leaves of the tree of life** (Revelation 22:2) who dwell among the **nations of the saved** (Revelation 21:24–26), rather than within the Bride (Revelation 21:9).

4. St. Clement of Alexandria (c. 150–215 C.E.)

Clement's words provide one of the clearest early affirmations of **post-mortem evangelism**—a concept distinct from universalism and yet possibly consistent with **non-elect salvation**. He presents the Gospel as preached not only to the living but also to **the dead**, even among **Gentiles** who did not hear the message during their earthly lives.

He writes:

> "Do not [the Scriptures] show that the Lord preached the Gospel to those that perished in the flood, or rather had been chained, and to those kept 'in ward and guard'? And it has been

shown also that the apostles, following the Lord, preached the Gospel to those in Hades... If, then, the Lord descended to Hades for no other end but to preach the Gospel... it was either for the sake of all, or certainly for the sake of those who had been better able to receive it."

This quote implies a possibility that **certain ones in Hades**—not all—were still reachable through the Gospel after death. These souls may not be part of **elect salvation**, for Clement doesn't declare they inherit eternal glory or reign with Christ, but they do appear to receive a salvific opportunity in the spirit realm. Thus, they could fall under a **non-elect salvific category**: **saved, but not glorified, delivered, but not crowned.**

5. St. John Chrysostom (c. 349–407 C.E.), Archbishop of Constantinople

Though Chrysostom does not teach a purgatorial fire or universal restoration, he allows space for the idea that some in Hades might ultimately be helped by the prayers of the righteous, even if they are not part of the elect. This creates a possible window into **non-elect salvation**—not based on earthly repentance but on mercy extended through intercessory remembrance.

In his *Homily on Philippians 1:1–2*, he writes:

"Not in vain was it decreed by the Apostles that in the dread Mysteries there should be a commemoration of the departed. They knew that great gain results to them, great benefit. For when the whole congregation stands with uplifted hands, and a priestly assembly, and that dread sacrifice is set forth, how shall we not prevail with God, entreating for them?"

While Chrysostom does not say these departed are ultimately saved into the **same glory** as the elect, he clearly teaches that they **benefit** and **are helped**—not by their own repentance but by the mercy extended through others' faith. If this intercessory help **alters their condition**, without bringing them into the elect inheritance, it closely aligns with the **non-elect salvific outcome**—a mercy extended posthumously, granting **relief or restoration** short of glorification.

6. St. Basil the Great (c. 330–379 C.E.), Bishop of Caesarea

St. Basil, one of the three Cappadocian Fathers, did not promote universalism, but like Chrysostom, he affirmed that intercessory prayer for the departed may be effective—even if the final result is not equal to the reward of the elect. He made room for **God's mercy** to operate beyond death in a manner that supports the possibility of **non-elect salvation.**

In his *Homily on Psalm 28*, he writes:

> "I know many who, after their departure from this life, have benefited from the prayers and the liturgy which is offered for them. I do not mean notorious sinners, but those who have committed minor faults and have gone to their rest, not altogether burdened by iniquities."

This clearly limits the help to those not "notorious sinners," but it implies that **departed souls,** already judged to some degree, may still be **relieved, helped, or shown mercy** through the intercessory acts of the Church. This **does not align with elect salvation**, which needs no after-death assistance, as Christ said of believers, "shall not come into judgment" (John 5:24). Therefore, if Basil's view is accurate, it opens the door to a **secondary category of salvation**—where some are **lifted out of punishment**, yet remain **outside the Tower**, meaning they do not inherit the elect's glorification.

7. St. Gregory of Nyssa (c. 335–c. 395 C.E.), younger brother of St. Basil the Great

St. Gregory of Nyssa is sometimes misunderstood as a universalist, but a careful reading shows that he differentiated between the **nature of divine justice** and the **purpose of post-mortem purification**. He envisioned a **long and painful purification** after death, not as eternal torment, but as a process that may restore certain souls—not all—to a level of righteousness.

In his work *On the Soul and the Resurrection*, he writes:

> "For evil must be entirely removed, and nothing left outside the limits of the good. And as long as anything is left in man of the mixture of evil, so long it is impossible for him to participate in the blessed life: we must be purged of the stains in a purifying fire."

This statement does **not affirm that all will be saved**, nor that this purification is reserved for Christians alone. Instead, Gregory envisions that **some souls**, even those **not in the Church**, may go through a **refining fire**, being purged until they are fit for some form of divine acceptance. This is not the **glorified state of the elect**, who are already judged faithful and rewarded at the First Resurrection (Revelation 20:6). Thus, Gregory's imagery matches the **Shepherd of Hermas' teaching** of a **"much inferior place"** for some souls after punishment, implying a **non-elect salvation possibility**.

8. St. Clement of Alexandria (c. 150–c. 215 C.E.)

St. Clement of Alexandria is one of the earliest and clearest voices in support of **post-mortem opportunities** for salvation—not for the elect, but possibly for those who had not responded properly to the Gospel in their earthly life. In *Stromata* (Book 6, Chapter 6), he writes:

> "Wherefore He [Christ] preached even to those in Hades, who had lived in ignorance, so that He might save all men, if possible, even among the Gentiles, through His appearing there also."

Clement's emphasis here is on **Christ preaching in Hades**, not merely to the Old Testament righteous, but even to **Gentiles who had lived in ignorance**. The phrase "if possible" leaves the outcome open—not guaranteeing universal salvation, but suggesting that **some among the ignorant**, even those who died without faith, might be granted mercy after judgment. That would make them candidates for **non-elect salvation**, as this mercy is not rooted in the rewards of faith or sanctification, but possibly in some earlier obedience to natural law or conscience (cf. Romans 2:14-16).

The elect are never said to be ignorant of Christ or the Gospel, nor are they said to come to faith in Hades. Clement's perspective acknowledges a **distinction between the elect who escape judgment (John 5:24) and others who may enter into judgment but receive mercy** through post-mortem means.

9. St. John of Damascus (c. 675–749 C.E.)

St. John of Damascus, though a later Church Father, offers intriguing comments in his *Exact Exposition of the Orthodox Faith* (Book IV, Chapter 27) that seem to align with a post-mortem preaching event not exclusively for the Old Testament righteous. He writes:

> "The Lord… came into Hades that He might bring out
> thence the souls of the righteous… But He did not rescue all, but
> only those who believed on Him."

Here, St. John affirms a **selective rescue** from Hades, not a universal one. Notably, he mentions those who believed on Him—not all of whom would have had the opportunity in life. The implication is that **belief occurred in Hades**, and only then were some released. This aligns with the idea that Christ's descent provided an opportunity for some to respond posthumously.

That kind of response cannot be classified as **elect salvation**, since elect believers are **never said to come into judgment or Hades** (John 5:24). Rather, those who are judged and then rescued after believing—post-mortem—would better fit a **non-elect salvation category**, as their deliverance is contingent upon belief after death, not before.

10. Clement of Alexandria (c. 150–c. 215 C.E.)

Clement of Alexandria stands out as one of the earliest and most developed theological voices to clearly propose a form of **post-mortem evangelism** and possible salvation for the dead. In his *Stromata* (Book VI, Chapter 6), Clement writes:

> "For the Gospel was preached even to those who were in
> Hades… And it was necessary that the best of the disciples should
> be imitators of their master; so those who had repented, though in
> Hades, were to be saved…"

Clement explicitly affirms the preaching of the Gospel in Hades and even says **repentance in Hades** could result in salvation. He is not merely speaking of the Old Testament saints but includes others who **repent in Hades**, implying they had formerly lived wicked lives or rejected the Gospel during their earthly lives.

This quote further supports the **non-elect salvation possibility** since these individuals are saved **after judgment begins in the spirit world**, not by faith in life. Clement distinguishes between those who are "elect" and those who "repent after death," affirming that **salvation is still attainable** for some through divine mercy beyond the grave—but apart from the Church and its sacraments.

11. St. John Chrysostom (c. 349–407 C.E.)

St. John Chrysostom, known for his strong homiletical style, acknowledges the mystery of divine mercy even in the afterlife. In his *Homily on Philippians 1:21–23*, he remarks:

> "Perhaps, indeed, many who are now in hell, the bottom of hell, may come into the kingdom; for God is mighty."

This statement is **not allegorical or poetic**, but part of Chrysostom's larger emphasis on **God's absolute power** to save whomever He wills—even from **the depths of Hades**. Chrysostom is not offering a guarantee but **opens the door** to hope for those currently under condemnation.

In the context of **non-elect salvation**, this quote may suggest that certain condemned persons—perhaps fallen believers, or unbelievers who showed mercy in life—could be **recipients of divine compassion posthumously**, though not inheriting the full privileges of the elect. He does not imply that all will be saved, nor does he offer a universalist view, but rather acknowledges **exceptions granted by God's sovereign mercy**.

12. St. Augustine of Hippo (354–430 C.E.)

Though often misunderstood as advocating a strict double-predestination model, St. Augustine made several nuanced remarks regarding God's dealings with the dead. One such passage comes from his *Enchiridion* (On Faith, Hope, and Love), where he considers the fate of those who were not reached by the Gospel:

> "For it is uncertain to whom God has willed to reveal this grace, and in what manner He dispenses it, especially in the case of infants, or of men who have not heard the Gospel and yet have lived in a manner that is not wholly dissolute."

This line reveals that Augustine **did not presume to limit God's mercy to a strict category of visible church members**. While he strongly affirms predestination and rejects universalism, he acknowledges the **possibility of God granting mercy to those outside the church**, particularly those who lived morally upright lives despite their ignorance of the Gospel.

In relation to **non-elect salvation**, this quote supports the idea that **God may extend a lesser or secondary salvation** to certain individuals who, while not part of the elect bride, still responded positively to the light of conscience or the law written in their hearts (Romans 2:14–16).

13. Clement of Alexandria (c. 150–c. 215 C.E.)

Clement provides one of the most direct patristic affirmations of post-mortem evangelism. In *Stromata* and *Who is the Rich Man That Shall Be Saved?*, he refers to the Gospel being preached to the dead, and he connects this directly to Christ's descent into Hades:

> "Do not [the Scriptures] show that the Lord preached the Gospel to those that perished in the flood, or rather had been shut up in Hades, and had been kept there until His descent, so that they might receive forgiveness and be saved?"

Clement's interpretation of 1 Peter 3:19 and related texts demonstrates his belief in **a salvation extended to certain dead souls in Hades**, which was not simply to condemn them but to offer hope. He reasons that God's justice demands such an opportunity:

> "How is it just that souls should perish without hearing the Word? It is not just. Therefore, the Gospel was preached also to the dead."

This early affirmation **undermines the idea that death irrevocably fixes one's eternal state** for all men. Clement opens the door to a **limited post-mortem salvation**—not for everyone, but perhaps for those who never had a genuine opportunity in life or who, though failing during their lifetime, could still respond after death.

In light of this, Clement becomes a credible historical witness to **non-elect salvation possibilities**, particularly in the Spirit World context—souls who receive grace not unto the bride's reward but unto some measure of mercy.

14. Origen of Alexandria (c. 185–c. 253 C.E.)

Origen is often misunderstood due to the later condemnations of some of his theological ideas, yet his writings remain among the most thorough explorations of post-mortem processes in early Christianity. In his *Commentary on Romans* and *Homilies on Jeremiah*, Origen taught that **some form of correction or purification continues after death:**

"When a soul leaves this world still having some stains, it must be purified before it can see God… this purification takes place through corrective punishments."

This is not Elect Salvation, which offers immediate entrance into the joy of the Lord and the First Resurrection reward. Rather, Origen's view implies a **gradual correction**, which could very well resemble the idea of **Non-Elect Salvation**—a mercy extended after judgment but outside the reward structure of the bride.

He writes in *Homily on Leviticus*:

"God descends even to hell to bring the Gospel to souls, that all may be judged, but some also saved."

Such teaching reflects 1 Peter 4:6, which says the Gospel was "preached even to the dead." Origen's universalism goes beyond the user's theological framework, but his **recognition that some could be saved post-mortem through repentance and divine mercy** aligns with a possible Non-Elect Salvation—especially for those not wicked to the core but still stained.

Origen's influence in Alexandrian theology, echoed in parts by Gregory of Nyssa later, means his statements should be taken seriously as patristic support for **Spirit World mercy**—though not automatic, and certainly not part of the Elect's glorification.

15. St. Clement of Alexandria (c. 150–c. 215 C.E.)

St. Clement, a teacher of Origen and head of the Catechetical School of Alexandria, provides one of the earliest recorded theological frameworks for a post-mortem evangelism directed at the **dead in Hades**. His teaching is rooted in 1 Peter 3:18–20 and 1 Peter 4:6, and he articulates a view that **some who died in ignorance of the Gospel receive an opportunity to believe after death**:

"Christ preached the Gospel to those in Hades… so that they might be judged according to men in the flesh, but live according to God in the spirit."

This aligns precisely with a Non-Elect Salvation framework. Clement distinguishes this class from those who are elect and saved in this life, suggesting that **God's mercy extends into the unseen realm**, but does not imply all will accept it.

In *Stromata* (Book VI), he affirms:

> "God's punishments are saving and disciplinary, leading to conversion, and choosing rather the repentance than the death of a sinner."

Again, this is not Elect Salvation which guarantees glorification and escape from judgment (John 5:24), but it does indicate a **graded post-mortem mercy** that may lead to salvation for some. He even believed that certain virtuous pagans—like Socrates and Heraclitus—had received a portion of the Logos and could be candidates for posthumous salvation:

> "It is not right to think that such men were without a portion of the Divine Logos."

This concept—that those who strove toward righteousness might yet receive light—echoes what we now define as Non-Elect Salvation. These souls would not be part of the Bride of Christ but could be among the saved "nations" who walk in the light of the New Jerusalem (Revelation 21:24).

16. Origen of Alexandria (c. 184–c. 253 C.E.)

Origen, a pupil of St. Clement, extended the Alexandrian framework with a detailed doctrine of **post-mortem discipline and correction**. While much of his speculative theology was condemned centuries later, his earlier writings—especially those preserved before the Fifth Ecumenical Council—carry great historical value and provide insight into early church speculation regarding the fate of souls after death.

Origen writes:

> "For the soul, after its departure from the world, shall be subjected to the punishment appropriate to its sins; this punishment is administered in proportion to the guilt and to the nature of the sins." (*De Principiis*, Book II.10)

This confirms a concept of **measured judgment** after death, not eternal torment for all, and supports the idea that some may pass through punishment to reach a form of salvation, especially if they were not part of the elect. Such souls, purified by fire, may be delivered—**but not to the Church's heavenly position**, and certainly not into the New Jerusalem. Origen holds that the ultimate purpose of judgment is not destruction, but **correction**.

He continues:

> "God's fire is not a consuming fire of annihilation but a refining fire that brings about moral purification."

While Origen's later universalism is rejected, the idea that **some receive salvation outside the Elect category**, especially after death and through judgment, fits the Non-Elect Salvation category. His image of **divine fire that disciplines and heals** resembles the picture in Revelation 22:2 of nations being healed—not glorified.

17. Didymus the Blind (c. 313–c. 398 C.E.)

Didymus the Blind, a leading theologian in Alexandria and successor to Origen's school, built upon many of Origen's theological trajectories. Though he rejected certain extremes, he still taught the possibility of post-mortem purgation and mercy, particularly for those not fully hardened in sin.

In his commentary, he writes:

> "The punishments of God are not inflicted to destroy but to convert the souls of those being punished. For even in Gehenna the correction is aimed at repentance, not vengeance." (*Commentary on Psalm 88*, fragment preserved by Jerome)

This quote is deeply aligned with the **Non-Elect Salvation** possibility. Didymus does not say this applies to the elect—who, as established earlier, are spared from such judgment (John 5:24). Rather, this applies to those who enter Gehenna but may still turn toward God **after punishment**, mirroring the Shepherd of Hermas' imagery of souls cast outside the tower yet permitted an inferior salvation.

Though later condemned alongside Origen, Didymus' view was not fringe in his time. He was respected by Athanasius and taught Jerome himself. The notion that punishment could bring about **repentance in the afterlife** for some—distinct from those who had full saving faith in Christ during their lives—strengthens the academic case for Non-Elect Salvation.

18. Diodore of Tarsus (d. c. 394 C.E.)

Diodore of Tarsus, a noted biblical scholar and head of the Antiochene school of theology, was known for his literal-historical approach to interpretation and for being the teacher of both John Chrysostom and Theodore of Mopsuestia. Though less speculative than Alexandrian theologians, Diodore also affirmed a distinction between varying degrees of postmortem judgment and hope.

In one preserved fragment, he comments:

> "Even after death, there is room for healing. For the Judge is just and also kind, and His judgments do not always end in destruction but in restoration, according to the measure of each." (Fragment cited in *Leontius of Byzantium, Against the Nestorians and Eutychians*, Book 2)

This idea opens a plausible line of interpretation in favor of **Non-Elect Salvation**, particularly in light of those whose deeds or moral conduct reflected godliness in part, yet without full knowledge of Christ or full repentance. His reference to **healing after death**—without tying it to full elect status—implies a secondary form of salvation, not identical to the glorified destiny of the church.

Though his writings are mostly lost, Diodore's legacy through his students shaped the theology of the Eastern Church. If this concept of **restorative judgment after death** for non-elect persons is rooted in the teachings of early respected scholars like him, it strengthens the historical witness that such a doctrine was contemplated within the boundaries of orthodoxy.

19. Theodore of Mopsuestia (c. 350–428 C.E.)

A prominent theologian of the Antiochene tradition, **Theodore of Mopsuestia** carried forward the historical-grammatical method of interpretation, inheriting it from his teacher Diodore of Tarsus. Though condemned posthumously in the 6th century for perceived Nestorianism, his influence on Eastern Christian thought was substantial. He, too, expressed a concept that opens the door to **Non-Elect Salvation**.

In his commentary on 1 Peter, preserved in part by later Syriac sources, he states:

> "The punishment of sinners in Gehenna is not eternal. It was designed for healing. The reason for this is so that the sins and evil that were in them may be utterly removed. For God is always seeking to bring His creatures back to what is better." (Cited in *Theodore of Mopsuestia: Commentary on the Minor Epistles*, Syriac fragments)

This notion of **punishment designed for healing**, not final destruction, reinforces the idea of **salvation after postmortem**

purification—not in the elect sense of glorification and co-reigning, but in a secondary form that results from divine mercy.

Theodore emphasizes that **God is always seeking the restoration** of His creation, which includes even those who enter the fires of judgment. This aligns with the **non-elect category**—those who undergo divine correction and, upon repentance, are granted a lesser form of salvation.

20. Didymus the Blind (c. 313–398 C.E.)

Didymus the Blind, a well-regarded theologian of the Alexandrian school and successor to Origen as head of the Catechetical School of Alexandria, offers statements that also align with the **Non-Elect Salvation** concept. Although he was later anathematized during the Second Council of Constantinople (553 C.E.) largely due to his perceived universalistic leanings inherited from Origen, his writings remained influential in early Christian theology.

In his treatise *On the Holy Spirit*, Didymus writes:

> "The punishments of hell are not eternal, they serve a disciplinary purpose. God, who created all, will eventually restore all His creatures to a state of harmony, after they have been purified through suffering."

This **non-final nature of punishment** again hints that **hell or Gehenna has a remedial purpose**, not necessarily retributive for all. While Didymus does not promote the **equal glorification** of all saved, his language suggests a **graded post-judgment salvation**—with those enduring disciplinary fires eventually being restored by God's mercy.

This idea reinforces the distinction between the **elect**, who escape judgment entirely (John 5:24), and those who must endure correction before possibly being saved in a **non-elect** capacity. It echoes earlier sentiments seen in the Shepherd of Hermas and 1 Enoch, where repentance is granted through suffering after judgment.

21. St. Gregory of Nyssa (c. 335–c. 395 C.E.)

St. Gregory of Nyssa, one of the three Cappadocian Fathers, wrote extensively on eschatology. While many of his statements are later cited by Universalists, we are here only highlighting selective portions that might be interpreted—without asserting universalism—as supportive of **Non-Elect Salvation**, especially in the context of **repentance after judgment** for some, but not necessarily all.

In his work *On the Soul and the Resurrection*, he states:

> "Being purified from evil, the soul begins to see the truth and, being thus led to the light, will then receive what is proper to its nature. For evil must be wholly removed, not as something which co-exists eternally with the good, but as something which is to be entirely removed and destroyed."

This echoes the pattern found in earlier testimonies: **post-mortem purification**, not in the church (Tower), and not in the elect class, but possibly for **a different order of salvation**—after judgment and fire. The language of "being thus led to the light" after purification implies **a transition from condemnation to restoration** that occurs **beyond this life**, thus corresponding to the **non-elect post-judgment salvation model**.

While Gregory's overall theology leaned toward universal restoration, this particular quote can be cautiously viewed within the framework of **limited, non-elect repentance after punishment**, without forcing it into the category of universal salvation. It remains consistent with the historical-grammatical possibility that **some may be saved after judgment but not as the elect**.

22. St. Basil the Great (c. 329–379 C.E.)

Though not as speculative in eschatology as his brother Gregory of Nyssa, St. Basil the Great, another of the Cappadocian Fathers, offers statements that could be understood as leaving space for **salvific mercy after death**—but not universally, and certainly not within the Elect class.

In *On the Holy Spirit* and various homilies, Basil defends the justice of God in punishing sin but also writes:

> "The punishment does not aim at revenge but at correction. It is the reformation of the soul, and the removal of defects."

This doctrine of **corrective chastisement**, rather than eternal torment, closely matches the concept of **non-elect salvation** following **post-mortem correction or refinement**. In this interpretive lens, Basil's theology allows for **some to be restored** after punishment, not because they were elect, but because the **disciplinary fire served its purpose** in bringing repentance.

Additionally, Basil upholds the **distinctive reward of the Elect**, making it improbable he saw all men reaching the same destiny. So if punishment can be restorative, and not everyone attains the highest glory, then **a lower tier of saved—outside the Tower, as Hermas would phrase it—remains a theological possibility.**

23. St. Gregory Nazianzen (c. 329–390 C.E.)

St. Gregory Nazianzen, also of the Cappadocian trio and honored as "The Theologian," makes a few key remarks that suggest **mercy beyond death for some**, particularly in the context of divine justice being tempered by love. His theology does not affirm universal salvation, but it provides hints of **hope for posthumous repentance** or change for certain souls.

In *Oration 45 (On Holy Pascha)*, he famously declares:

> "God will not be overcome by evil. He overcomes evil with good. For God punishes not for punishment's sake, but for correction's."

While this statement upholds the reality of divine punishment, it presents that punishment as **corrective, not retributive**, suggesting some degree of hope beyond immediate condemnation. This fits the concept that **non-elect persons**, after having faced divine correction in the afterlife (such as Hades or the Lake of Fire), **might still attain a form of salvation— though not the glorious reward of the Elect.**

Gregory never teaches universalism. His emphasis remains on **repentance**, holiness, and the final judgment. But by portraying punishment as reformative, not final in nature for all, he permits a **non-elect salvation category**—reserved for the corrected, not the unrepentant.

24. St. Ephraim the Syrian (c. 306–373 C.E.)

St. Ephraim, one of the greatest theologians and hymnographers of the Syriac-speaking church, often expressed deep reverence for divine justice and mercy, sometimes envisioning **posthumous pardon** in poetic and meditative language. His insights are not systematic doctrine, but his expressions do reflect **occasional hope for souls beyond death.**

In one of his *Hymns on Paradise* (Hymn VII), he writes:

> "Perhaps the sinful will be scourged for a time, and after they have been tormented, they will be released."

Though St. Ephraim does not teach eternal security or universal redemption, this statement recognizes a **temporary punishment** in the afterlife—scourging or torment—**after which release is possible.** Such language strongly supports the concept that **some sinners endure a limited post-death judgment, yet are not eternally lost.**

This "release" is not into the same glory as the Elect but implies a **non-elect category of salvation**—souls who did not live up to the elect standard but were ultimately not forsaken due to God's enduring compassion.

25. St. Macarius the Great (c. 300–391 C.E.)

St. Macarius, an Egyptian desert father known for his spiritual depth and practical holiness, presents some remarkable thoughts in his homilies that have implications for the **possibility of posthumous repentance or cleansing**—though, like earlier fathers, he speaks in a spiritual-mystical tone rather than formal doctrinal structure.

In *Homily 43*, attributed to Macarius, we read:

> "If those in Gehenna, even there, would repent with their whole heart, and call upon God, He would have mercy on them… even in hell, the compassionate God would accept their repentance."

This profound remark explicitly states a **possibility of mercy extended even in Gehenna**, not based on a pre-death repentance but on **repentance that could occur in the afterlife**. This cannot be speaking of the elect, who are not judged in Gehenna, but instead refers to **non-elect persons enduring judgment** who might yet respond rightly.

The implication is that while punishment is real, and divine justice is uncompromising, **the door of divine mercy remains unlocked**, provided the heart genuinely turns toward God. This aligns with the **Non-Elect Salvation** model—individuals outside the elect group, judged in the spirit world, yet shown mercy if they eventually repent under that judgment.

26. St. Isaac of Nineveh (c. 613–c. 700 C.E.)

St. Isaac the Syrian, also known as Isaac of Nineveh, offers some of the most spiritually penetrating and compassionate reflections ever written in patristic literature. Though writing centuries after the earlier fathers and from a monastic perspective, his words are often considered **a window into deeper possibilities of God's dealings with souls**, especially in the context of divine mercy.

He writes:

> "As a handful of sand thrown into the great sea, so are the sins of all flesh in comparison with the mind of God—and as a strongly flowing fountain is not obstructed by a handful of dust, so the compassion of the Creator is not conquered by the wickedness of his creatures."

St. Isaac's expression affirms that God's **mercy is so infinitely vast** that even **the greatest accumulation of sin does not obstruct His compassion**. While this statement does not explicitly reference Hades or the Lake of Fire, it fits the theological architecture of **Non-Elect Salvation**: that there could be souls judged and punished in the afterlife whose wickedness is eventually overcome by God's overflowing compassion if they turn.

St. Isaac does not define who these persons are, nor does he call them the elect. His focus is instead on the **boundless scope of divine love and its potential to reach beyond time and judgment**, which again supports this category of **salvation through post-judgment repentance**, consistent with the possibility that **some non-elect may be saved after Spirit World judgment**.

27. St. Macarius the Great (c. 300–c. 391 C.E.)

St. Macarius of Egypt, a desert father and monastic leader, is often cited for his deeply mystical and pastoral writings, some of which imply a broader vision of God's redemptive plan. In one of his attributed homilies, Macarius reflects on the **transforming power of divine light**, even toward those in judgment:

> "There is within the heart a place of burning, and there is also a place of light. The Lord comes, even to the lowest and darkest places, to awaken the soul."

While this is not an explicit doctrinal claim about salvation from Hades or Gehenna, Macarius seems to teach that **God's Spirit is not bound**, and that **divine illumination can reach even the most hidden places within the soul**—places associated with darkness, bondage, and perhaps even postmortem condemnation.

By framing the heart as containing both a "place of burning" and "a place of light," he introduces a conceptual dualism that **may symbolize earthly and post-earthly chastisement and renewal**, respectively. His claim that "the Lord comes... even to the lowest and darkest places" resonates with the idea that **God's mercy may penetrate realms like Hades**, offering a chance for awakening.

Again, this is not elect salvation. The elect are said to be fully transformed at the first resurrection and do not experience darkness or punishment (cf. Revelation 20:6). But if St. Macarius is speaking about a **later illumination** for those in the depths—especially in a context of purifying fire—it aligns with the framework of **non-elect salvation** as a **post-judgment mercy** granted to some souls.

28. St. Gregory of Nazianzus (c. 329–c. 390 C.E.)

St. Gregory of Nazianzus, one of the most revered Cappadocian Fathers, offers a particularly remarkable statement in his **Oration 45**, delivered on the occasion of Easter. He affirms Christ's descent into Hades and expands the implications of this act with a notable openness:

> "Perhaps He is even now purifying you in fire, in this fire which is not eternal but for a time, which is wisely applied, as He who is the Judge, knowing the reasons for things, applies it."

This statement from Gregory clearly distinguishes between **eternal condemnation** and a **temporary purifying fire**. His use of the phrase "not eternal but for a time" strongly suggests that **some souls endure a remedial form of judgment**, not as final damnation, but as purification. Importantly, he asserts that this purgative fire is administered **wisely** by the Judge who "knows the reasons," hinting at **divine equity** and the potential for redemption even beyond death.

Gregory does not place such souls within the church or the resurrection of the just, and thus this idea is best understood as **non-elect salvation**—a temporary punishment culminating in mercy, not the glorified status of the elect.

His view does not support universalism either, because he restricts this mercy to some and still affirms that for others the fire could be eternal. Yet for those judged worthy of purgation, Gregory allows the possibility of restoration—a thought compatible with the **non-elect saved** category who are purified, then granted some form of post-resurrection life outside the heavenly city.

29. St. Basil the Great (c. 329–379 C.E.)

St. Basil, the brother of Gregory of Nyssa and a close associate of Gregory of Nazianzus, also appears to leave room for a tiered view of postmortem outcomes. In his **Homily on Psalm 28 (29)**, he states:

"When the just Judge shall sit, He will weigh our deeds, and will give to each his due: some He will purify here, others there, so that they may be saved as by fire."

This phrase, "so that they may be saved as by fire," draws from 1 Corinthians 3:15 and mirrors the earlier interpretation found in both **Gregory of Nazianzus** and **Origen**, though Basil is more restrained than Origen. He does not state that **all** will be purified or saved, but that **some** may be saved in a fiery way—a clear implication of a **non-elect salvation** scenario.

Basil does not teach universal salvation, but he does point out a **difference in judgment and outcome**, depending on each person's deeds. The ones "purified there"—meaning in the spirit world or postmortem context—are not counted among the elect who reign, but possibly among the saved who must undergo temporal punishment.

Basil's language is not speculative. He speaks with pastoral certainty that **God's justice is not arbitrary**, but proportionate and reformative for some. This fits the model of those saved outside the Church's Tower, placed in a lower but still redemptive state—not in Heaven, but spared from everlasting destruction.

30. St. John Chrysostom (c. 347–407 C.E.)

St. John Chrysostom, famed for his bold preaching and theological clarity, while often interpreted as a staunch defender of strict judgment, nonetheless offers a significant window into a potential **non-elect salvation** when he reflects on 1 Corinthians 3:15. In his **Homilies on the Epistle to the Corinthians**, he interprets Paul's phrase, "he himself shall be saved, yet so as by fire," as follows:

"For he indeed is saved, yet so as by fire: that is, with difficulty. For it is impossible for a man, who has led a careless life, immediately to be made equal to him who has lived with exactness. He saves him, but he saves him thus, as by fire, cutting off his pleasures, and compelling him to suffer things grievous."

Here Chrysostom affirms that **salvation may occur through suffering** and divine chastisement. Importantly, this chastisement is **not annihilation** nor a punitive damnation but a means of **purging sin and instilling righteousness**—echoing the Shepherd of Hermas' depiction of "repenting in fire of punishment" and being placed in a lower, non-elect category.

He distinguishes between those who lived righteously and those who were careless or sluggish in their walk, stating that the careless may still be saved—but not in the same way or to the same glory as the faithful. That implies a **graded eschatology**, with some saved into a lower glory or position, distinct from the first resurrection elect.

31. St. Basil the Great (c. 330–379 C.E.)

St. Basil, a central Cappadocian Father, addresses divine judgment and mercy in his **Homily on Psalm 33**, where he reflects on the suffering endured by the wicked and the possibility of eventual restoration:

> "The tribulations which are inflicted for healing purposes are not punishments properly speaking, but chastisements and corrections administered for the sake of salvation. Just as in the case of bodies that are diseased, cauterization and surgery are applied not to destroy but to save life, so the evils that come upon sinners are meant to convert the soul."

Though St. Basil does not explicitly refer to salvation after death or in Hades, this quote underscores a theological principle that aligns with **non-elect salvation** possibility: namely, that **punishments from God may serve to correct, not to condemn**. His analogy to surgery suggests an ultimately restorative purpose behind divine discipline, even if it is severe.

The implication is that **some sinners, even after temporal judgment, may be led to repentance and salvation**, though not necessarily into the elect glory of the Church. This echoes the Shepherd of Hermas and 1 Enoch's presentation of **post-judgment repentance through suffering**, possibly pointing to a **non-elect category of salvation** consistent with chiliasm.

32. St. Gregory of Nyssa (c. 335–c. 395 C.E.)

St. Gregory of Nyssa, the younger brother of St. Basil, provides one of the clearest Patristic articulations that might support a **non-elect salvation** model—especially in his theological reflections on postmortem purification. In his work *On the Soul and the Resurrection*, he states:

> "Being purged of evil by suffering, in proportion as it deserves to be cleansed, the soul will be restored to its original condition of purity. For if evil is a disease of the soul, and if disease does not

remain in the body after health has been restored, then neither will evil remain in the soul after the expulsion of its impurity."

Gregory speaks in metaphor, comparing the soul's corruption to a disease and envisioning its eventual healing through suffering. The implication is that **some souls—though not numbered among the elect in the first resurrection—may still be purged and saved in a different capacity**.

This purification, unlike the full reward of the saints, does not restore honor or status but simply **cleanses to a basic state of life**. That would match the proposed category of **non-elect salvation—a salvation that occurs **after judgment** and via suffering, not in the honor of the Church but still granted by God's grace and mercy.

33. St. Basil the Great (c. 330–379 C.E.)

St. Basil the Great, though renowned for his defense of orthodox doctrine and the reality of eternal punishment, leaves room for interpretative nuance in his remarks about the purification of certain souls. In his *Homily on Psalm 28 (29)*, Basil suggests:

> "In the fear of the Lord is a confidence of strength. That fear is not without purpose which teaches us to avoid punishment, for it is by this fear that some are brought to compunction and repentance. And the fire of judgment, which devours the adversaries, is not without the purification of those who are saved by fire."

While he does affirm judgment fire "devours adversaries," he also makes a distinction, saying **some are saved by fire**. Basil references 1 Corinthians 3:15, where a man's work is burned but he himself is saved "yet so as through fire." This allows for a salvation that follows judgment, not preceding it, and **not necessarily within the elect Tower or Church context**.

Thus, Basil's acknowledgment that some may be "saved by fire" without enjoying the reward of the faithful aligns with the **possibility of a non-elect salvation**—souls who are not cast into final destruction but undergo postmortem purification apart from the glory and inheritance of the saints.

34. Gregory of Nyssa (c. 335–c. 395 C.E.)

Gregory of Nyssa presents one of the more striking testimonies among the Church Fathers when discussing postmortem purification, which may coincide with the non-elect salvation model. In his *On the Soul and the Resurrection*, Gregory writes:

> "When, after long periods of time, evil has been eradicated, and the nature of all things restored to its original condition, then God will be all in all... [and] every soul shall be united to the blessedness of the Divine life."

Although some interpreters use this passage to promote universalism, Gregory does not explicitly deny judgment, punishment, or hellfire. What is noteworthy is that he speaks of **souls being eventually united with divine life after purification**, even if their initial path was one of rejection or judgment.

He also says:

> "For the soul that has turned away from the good and become rooted in the material and the sensual must be purged by suffering, in order that it may be restored to its original condition."

This suggests that **restoration** after suffering is possible—not restoration to elect reward or church inheritance, but **restoration to a lower form of life in submission to divine order**. Such statements do not imply equality of salvation with the elect but may reflect **a lesser, purified state consistent with non-elect salvation**, especially if one distinguishes between entering the New Heavens versus the New Earth (Revelation 21:1, 24–27).

35. Didymus the Blind (c. 313–398 C.E.)

Didymus the Blind, a student of Origen and one of the leading theologians of the Alexandrian tradition, also expressed thoughts that align with the idea of postmortem salvation—not necessarily for the elect, but for certain judged souls who are purified through divine justice.

In his commentary on 1 Peter (fragmentary), Didymus writes:

> "The punishments of God are salvific and not purely retributive, for correction, not for destruction. Even those cast into Gehenna are not beyond the reach of divine mercy."

This view is not equivalent to elect salvation as described in John 5:24 or Revelation 20:6, where there is **no second death** and **no judgment** for those counted worthy in Christ. Rather, Didymus recognizes that **some souls undergo divine punishment after death**, but **eventually are restored** by God's mercy. That qualifies as **postmortem redemption or rehabilitation**, but not as reward inheritance or kingdom reign.

In another passage (cited by Jerome in *Epistle 84*), Didymus suggests that:

> "Even the devil may eventually be saved."

Although that particular statement was later condemned, the broader context shows Didymus's belief that **no soul is beyond divine correction**. Theologically, this may open the possibility of **non-elect salvation**—not a restoration to glory, but an escape from final ruin for some, after fire and chastisement.

36. Jerome (c. 347–420 C.E.)

While Jerome is often more cautious than Origen or Didymus, even he occasionally speaks of divine mercy extending beyond this life—not in a way that affirms universal salvation, but in ways that acknowledge **degrees of punishment** and the **possibility of redemption** for some souls after death.

In his commentary on Isaiah 66:24, Jerome notes:

> "Some will be saved by fire. Not all who are judged are consumed forever, but some are healed through punishment, as gold is refined in a furnace."

Here, Jerome echoes the metaphor of purification through fire—similar to 1 Corinthians 3:15, which speaks of a man whose work is burned, "yet he himself will be saved, yet so as through fire." In Jerome's understanding, this **fire is not eternal torment for all**, but functions as a **means of correction for some**.

This does not align with the first resurrection elect who avoid judgment entirely (John 5:24; Revelation 20:6). Rather, it may be seen as a class of **souls judged but not ultimately condemned**, possibly pointing to the **non-elect** being refined and spared final destruction.

37. Augustine of Hippo (354–430 C.E.)

Though Augustine is a foundational theologian for the doctrine of eternal punishment, he also acknowledges that **not all punishment is everlasting**. While he firmly rejects the universalist view of Origen, he still admits that **some souls may be saved after temporal chastisement**, suggesting a category that could fit the non-elect salvation possibility.

In *Enchiridion on Faith, Hope, and Love*, Augustine writes:

> "Some men will be saved by fire: not that they escape pain, but that their pain leads to purification."

He comments further:

> "There are some who are not so wicked as to deserve to be damned forever, nor yet so good as to be admitted at once to the fellowship of the blessed."

This nuanced view—recognizing a **middle category of souls** neither fully wicked nor fully righteous—leaves space for a **post-mortem purification** that does not belong to the elect (who face no condemnation, John 5:24), nor the reprobate (who are permanently condemned). If such individuals are purified and eventually saved, **not into the elect position**, but into a **lesser estate**, this could align with the **non-elect salvation possibility** being discussed.

38. Jerome (c. 347–420 C.E.)

Jerome, the translator of the Latin Vulgate and a formidable biblical scholar, also hints at a **post-mortem salvific possibility** for some souls. While not stating it dogmatically, he acknowledges the idea that **some souls undergo punishment temporarily and are later released**, though not necessarily into the glory reserved for the saints.

In his commentary on Isaiah 66:24, which describes the fire and worm of the damned, Jerome remarks:

> "This does not mean they are forever tormented, but for a long time, as it were without end, according to the duration appropriate for the measure of their sins."

Though Jerome doesn't define their final state as heavenly, his words open the possibility that **not all punishment is eternal** and that **some are corrected or purged** proportionately. This matches well with a **non-elect**

salvation that follows divine justice yet grants **a future escape from condemnation without the full privileges of elect glory**.

39. Augustine of Hippo (354–430 C.E.)

Although Augustine is typically cited as the strong voice for the eternality of punishment, **there are early traces in his writings that reveal nuance** regarding the finality and equality of all punishments in hell. In particular, his earlier work *Enchiridion on Faith, Hope, and Love* includes a passage that many have cited as indicative of **some form of graded mercy**, even if not for the elect:

> "But temporary punishments are suffered by some in this life only, by others after death, by others both now and then; but all of them before that last and strictest judgment. Yet not all who are to suffer temporary punishments shall afterwards be delivered from them."

Here Augustine acknowledges **temporary punishments after death** that precede the final judgment, with a suggestion that **some will be delivered**, even though not all. He distinguishes between these temporary punishments and the final "strictest judgment," which corresponds to the **Lake of Fire** in Revelation. This may indicate **a Spirit World judgment in Hades** that **some are delivered from**, echoing the **non-elect salvation model**—distinct from those who are delivered unto everlasting life as the elect.

40. Augustine of Hippo (continued)

In *City of God*, Book XXI, Chapter 13, Augustine again touches on the nature of future punishment, but with a subtle distinction that could allow for non-elect salvation in rare cases. He writes:

> "There are some, indeed, who suppose that those who are to be thus punished will, after a time, be delivered from their sufferings… whose opinion, if not true, is certainly merciful."

Although he ultimately rejects this idea in favor of the traditional eternal punishment view for the reprobate, he does not label the merciful position heretical or unorthodox. Rather, he calls it "certainly merciful." This might suggest that **even Augustine was open to the concept in theory**, even if not embracing it doctrinally.

Therefore, in this early development of Western theology, **Augustine preserves language that hints at temporary postmortem suffering** from which **some might be delivered**, which **aligns loosely with the concept of non-elect salvation through Spirit World judgment and repentance**—though he personally preferred the stricter eternal model.

41. Augustine of Hippo (final related note)

In *Enchiridion on Faith, Hope and Love*, Chapter 112, Augustine speaks about those who are saved "as by fire," referencing 1 Corinthians 3:15:

> "Some shall be saved, yet so as by fire... they shall be saved indeed, but only so as through fire. That is, they shall be saved indeed, but it shall be as by fire; for their building has not been of the best materials."

Augustine applies this to Christians whose works are lacking, yet who are still saved. Although this primarily relates to the elect, **the principle that one can be saved after passing through divine fire** adds **a foundational idea that may support** the framework of **non-elect salvation**, particularly for those who did not walk rightly but still responded to truth imperfectly.

This supports the idea that fire may be a **refining, not annihilating**, force for some—**a necessary trial** for entrance into a **lesser salvation state**, which aligns with the Shepherd of Hermas imagery of a **"much more inferior place"** for those who are not part of the elect "Tower."

42. Conclusion to Patristic Survey in Essay 9

From these multiple sources—ranging from apocalyptic literature (*1 Enoch*), early Christian visions (*Shepherd of Hermas*), and prominent patristic writers (St. Ambrose, Clement of Alexandria, Origen, Methodius, Gregory of Nyssa, and even Augustine)—a recurring pattern is observed: **repentance and salvation extended beyond this life in certain exceptional cases.** While these cases do not align with **Elect Salvation**, which avoids any Spirit World judgment altogether (John 5:24; Revelation 2:11), they imply a **postmortem salvific hope** distinct from the rewards and resurrection of the righteous.

Most notably, **non-elect salvation** is never described with the **same glory, authority, or intimacy** reserved for the elect in the first resurrection. Instead, it's always spoken of as **lesser in honor**, often following **divine punishment, repentance, or acknowledgment of truth** after seeing judgment. This category could include righteous Gentiles, those who faltered yet retained some charity, or those who heard the Gospel yet drew back.

The **church fathers themselves never claimed** these were the same as those who reigned with Christ. Instead, they left open the possibility of **salvation for some souls after judgment**, though **not within the Church**, and always **by God's mercy, not covenantal promise.**

CHAPTER 10 Baptism by Fire

St. Justin of Rome appears to classify mankind into **three distinct categories—the righteous (Christians), sinners, and the wicked—** rather than the more commonly assumed dichotomy of just righteous versus wicked. This triadic view aligns with a lesser-discussed biblical verse that reads, "Be kind and merciful, as your Father also is kind and merciful, and makes His sun to rise on **sinners**, and the **righteous**, and the **wicked**." Such a division opens the door to a possible interpretive model where **sinners may be saved by fire, the wicked remain unsaved**, and **the righteous are saved without judgment**. This interpretive proposal is offered as a framework for understanding the **Baptism of Fire**, mentioned in Matthew 3.

The principal passage for this doctrine reads, "I indeed baptize you with water unto repentance, but He who is coming after me is mightier than I, whose sandals I am not worthy to carry. He will baptize you with the Holy Spirit and fire. His winnowing fan is in His hand, and He will thoroughly clean out His threshing floor, and gather His wheat into the barn; but He will burn up the chaff with unquenchable fire." This verse contains both mercy and judgment: wheat gathered safely, while chaff is consumed.

St. Gregory Nazianzus' interpretation of 1 Corinthians 3:15—"If anyone's work is burned, he will suffer loss; but he himself will be saved, yet so as through fire"—is especially relevant. Gregory links this passage to **Novation heretics**, who rejected the mainstream Church and followed their own path. He refers to this process as a **"last Baptism,"** one more painful and prolonged than earthly baptism. His words are striking: "Let these men then if they will, follow our way, which is Christ's way; but if they will not, let them go their own. **Perhaps in it they will be baptized with Fire**, in that last Baptism which is more painful and longer, which devours wood like grass and consumes the stubble of every evil."

This fire, being connected with 1 Corinthians 3, is not for the elect— who have already passed from death into life without condemnation (John 5:24)—but for those who went astray or resisted Christ's path. Therefore, if these are saved by fire, it can only be as a **non-elect salvation** scenario. Gregory differentiates this further by describing **two fires**: a **cleansing fire** for some, and an **avenging fire** for others. In his words: "For I know a cleansing fire which Christ came to send upon the earth, and He Himself is analogically called a Fire… For all these belong to the destroying power; **though some may prefer even in this place to take a more merciful view of this fire, worthily of Him That chastises.**"

Then Gregory plainly outlines the other type: "I know also a fire which is not cleansing, but avenging; either that fire of Sodom which He pours down on all sinners, mingled with brimstone and storms, or that which is prepared for the Devil and his Angels, or that which proceeds from the face of the Lord, and shall burn up his enemies round about; and one even more fearful still than these, the unquenchable fire which is ranged with the worm that dieth not but is eternal for the wicked. **For all these belong to the destroying power.**"

In summary, **Gregory's distinction** between a cleansing fire and an avenging fire opens up the conceptual space for non-elect individuals—specifically heretics and perhaps even unbelievers—to be saved by fire through chastisement. This cleansing fire, though not for the righteous, still preserves some from eternal ruin, provided they are not hardened and damned like the wicked. Such a possibility, implied in the patristic text and harmonized with Scripture, points to a **non-elect salvation** occurring **after Spirit World Judgment.**

Among the principal Chiliast Church Fathers, **St. Justin of Rome** offers a critical witness regarding the **Judgment of Fire** spoken of in **Matthew 3:11–12**. He affirms that this fiery baptism is associated with the **Second Coming of Christ**, not the First. He cites the familiar prophetic declaration made by John the Baptist: "I baptize you with water to repentance; but He that is stronger than I shall come, whose shoes I am not worthy to bear: He shall baptize you with the Holy Ghost and with fire: whose fan is in His hand, and He will thoroughly purge His floor, and will gather the wheat into the barn; but the chaff He will burn up with unquenchable fire."

St. Justin explains that this prophecy pertains to the **second advent**, stating plainly: "For the prophets have proclaimed two advents of His: the one, that which is already past, when He came as a dishonoured and suffering Man; but the second, when, according to prophecy, **He shall come from heaven with glory**, accompanied by His angelic host, when also **He shall raise the bodies of all men who have lived**, and shall **clothe those of the worthy with immortality**, and **shall send those of the wicked, endued with eternal sensibility, into everlasting fire** with the wicked devils."

This placement of judgment at the Second Coming is significant because, according to St. Justin's Chiliasm framework, there is a **clear thousand-year interval** between the **First Resurrection** (for the elect) and the **general resurrection** (for all others). He writes: "But I and others, who are right-minded Christians on all points, are assured that there will be a **resurrection of the dead, and a thousand years in Jerusalem**, which will then be built, adorned, and enlarged, [as] the prophets Ezekiel and Isaiah and others declare… and that thereafter the general, and, in short, the **eternal resurrection and judgment of all men** would likewise take place."

Therefore, in light of St. Justin's own eschatological sequence, **Matthew 3:11–12** and its imagery of fiery judgment may point not to the final resurrection of the body, but to a **Spirit World judgment occurring between the two resurrections**. The **wheat gathered into the barn** may refer to the elect, while the **chaff burned with unquenchable fire** could symbolize the wicked. If any among the "chaff" are later redeemed through the cleansing process implied by "fire," this would not be the elect—who have no condemnation (John 5:24)—but a **different class entirely**, fitting the model of **non-elect salvation**.

St. Justin strengthens this timeline with another profound statement concerning the final transformation of the faithful. In explaining Psalm 82:1—"God stands in the congregation of gods; He judges among the gods"—he notes that these "gods" are the glorified Christians, those transformed after the Second Resurrection. He writes: "Listen, sirs, how the Holy Ghost speaks of this people, saying that they are all sons of the Highest; and how this very Christ will be present in their assembly, rendering judgment to all men." This occurs after the Millennium and demonstrates that even among the saved, there are ranks and moments of transformation—only **those who dwell with Christ during the 1000 years receive the highest glory** of being His Bride, while others, raised after, may obtain life in some **secondary or lesser state**.

Thus, if any are purified by fire between the First and Second Resurrections, yet not glorified as the elect, they would necessarily belong to the **non-elect**—and their salvation, while real, would be of **a lower inheritance**, outside the blessings of the first resurrection and millennial reign.

Tertullian draws a stark distinction between those who are **truly saved Christians** and those who merely **appear to believe**, affirming that **no true Christian**—that is, one possessing a stable and genuine faith—is baptized in fire. Rather, he explains that fire baptism is reserved for those whose **faith is**

weak or pretended, linking this to a **judgment** context, not to reward. He writes: *"True and stable faith is baptized with water, unto salvation; pretended and weak faith is baptized with fire, unto judgment."* This suggests that fire is not part of the believer's sanctification but instead a form of punitive or corrective judgment—most likely experienced in the **Spirit World** and not in this life.

If so, then anyone saved **after** enduring this fiery baptism could not belong to the elect. According to the Gospel parable of the sower, even the **minimum thirtyfold fruit-bearing** believer—defined as "good ground"—is not portrayed as going through such post-mortem judgment (Mark 4:8). In that light, those judged by fire and yet saved may be **non-elect** individuals. Tertullian's identification of "pretended" faith with fire judgment also raises the point: how can one have 'pretended faith' and still be regarded as elect? The implication is that such souls might **not be believers at all**, yet could still be refined and saved through post-mortem fire—matching the idea of **Non-Elect Salvation.**

This interpretation gains additional weight from another statement in which Tertullian outlines a Spirit World judgment scenario. He warns that the Judge may *"commit you to the prison of hell, out of which there will be no dismissal until the smallest even of your delinquencies be paid off in the period before the resurrection."* This describes a temporary judgment—not eternal damnation—but one which only ends at the **resurrection**, implying that a soul may emerge from hell cleansed, but only **after** enduring punishment.

Whereas other Church Fathers like **St. Irenaeus** seem to suggest that the **last trumpet** (1 Corinthians 15:52) or **John 5:28–29** may refer only to one general resurrection of both the righteous and the wicked, Tertullian uniquely maintains a **gradual resurrection** model. He believes that **Christians themselves rise at different times during the 1000 years**, depending on merit. He states, *"Within [the thousand years] is completed the resurrection of the saints, who rise sooner or later according to their deserts."* This means that **not all elect rise together**, and some may rise quite late—perhaps even at the end of the 1000 years.

But such a model raises a problem. Those who rise at the end of the Millennium would necessarily **miss the Marriage Supper of the Lamb**, which concludes with the close of the 1000 years (Revelation 19:7–9). This absence disqualifies them from being **part of the Bride**, which Scripture clearly identifies as those who are ready at Christ's return (cf. Matthew 25:10). Therefore, Tertullian's model—despite assigning late resurrection to weak or carnal believers—suggests these are not part of the elect. His further statements imply that even some **souls rescued from Hades** will be transformed after resurrection: *"He who has already traversed Hades is destined also to obtain the change after the resurrection… the flesh will by all means rise again, and… assume the condition of angels."*

If so, these individuals are not glorified with the first group of saints but still **obtain life**, being changed into immortality—an event he links to **John 5:28–29**. Tertullian reads that passage **literally** and **without separating it into two resurrections** spaced a thousand years apart: *"All that are in the graves shall hear the voice of the Son of God, and shall come forth: they that have done good, to the resurrection of life; and they that have done evil, unto the resurrection of damnation."* He emphasizes that these refer to literal bodily graves and not merely allegorical "states."

Finally, Tertullian affirms that **flesh and blood cannot inherit the kingdom of God**, not because of their substance, but because of sin. Yet even those who rise for judgment—not kingdom—will still rise in the flesh: *"There is even a confirmation of the general resurrection of the flesh, whenever a special one is excepted… while it is in consideration of men's merits that a difference is made in their resurrection by their conduct in the flesh."* Thus, those who are not eligible for the kingdom may still be **resurrected**, experience **Spirit World judgment**, and possibly be **saved**, though not as the Elect.

This amounts to a strong Patristic witness from Tertullian that **Non-Elect Salvation** is at least **possible**, through a post-mortem purgative judgment, distinct from the elect's glorification and exclusion from wrath.

St. Irenaeus of Lyons affirms only **two advents of Christ**, directly opposing modern **pre-tribulation rapture** theories that insert a secret coming. He identifies **Matthew 3:11–12's Judgment of Fire** with the **Second Coming**, when Christ returns in power to "cleanse His floor." This language strongly indicates that the "baptism by fire" begins its work at the Second Coming—not as an invisible rapture but as a visible and world-shaking event. He writes that Christ will come *"bringing on the day which burns as a furnace… having a fan in His hands, and cleansing His floor, and gathering the wheat indeed into His barn, but burning the chaff with unquenchable fire"*.

This shows a **dual effect** of that fire: **gathering the wheat** (clearly believers) and **burning the chaff** (clearly the wicked). However, the phrase "cleansing His floor" indicates the beginning of a **process** rather than an immediate and total separation. This opens a possibility that some among the "chaff" might still be **purged** and later gathered—not in the Elect's resurrection, but in a later stage. The fire, in this case, may not be entirely destructive—it may have a **purification function** for some, especially when considered alongside other Church Fathers who speak of post-mortem cleansing.

Irenaeus then outlines how the **First Resurrection** begins right after Christ **destroys the Antichrist**, initiating the **Millennial reign**. He explains: *"Then the Lord will come from heaven… sending this man [the Antichrist] and those who follow him into the lake of fire; but bringing in for the righteous the times of the kingdom, that is, the rest, the hallowed seventh day."* This kingdom is the promised **Millennial Sabbath**, a 1000-year reign on earth in which only the righteous—those who take part in the First Resurrection—will live and reign with Christ (Revelation 20:4–6).

But the fact that Christ **begins** to cleanse His floor during His Second Coming leaves open the idea that not all are immediately cast into final fire. The imagery of **wheat and chaff** does not conclude at the Second Coming but begins then. The implication is that the sorting of mankind includes **layers** of judgment and purification, which is consistent with a **Non-Elect Salvation possibility**—especially for those not found worthy to rise at the first resurrection but who may still be saved later.

This timeline is further clarified when Irenaeus distinguishes between the **Millennial kingdom** and the **New Heavens and New Earth**. He explains that the **fashion of this world passes away** after the Millennium is complete. The *new Jerusalem* descends only then. He writes: *"When these things… pass away above the earth, John… says that the new Jerusalem above shall [then] descend, as a bride adorned for her husband… and that this is the tabernacle of God, in which God will dwell with men."* The old Jerusalem, where the saints reign during the Millennium, is only a **type**—a **disciplinary arena**—in which the righteous are prepared for incorruption.

Notice that **nothing is allegorized**. He explicitly rejects symbolic or spiritualized interpretations: *"Nothing is capable of being allegorized, but all things are steadfast, and true, and substantial."* This means that the **purification**, the **Millennial kingdom**, and the **new Jerusalem** are all understood as literal, progressive realities. First comes the **destruction of the Antichrist**, then the **resurrection of the righteous**, then **purification and discipline** during the Millennium, and finally, after all things are made new, **eternal life in the city of God**.

This order of events lends weight to the idea that **not all purification is complete at the Second Coming**. Rather, Christ's act of *cleansing His floor* might stretch across time during the 1000 years—especially for those outside the first resurrection. While the Elect are gathered into the barn immediately (Luke 3:17), the rest may undergo fiery judgment or discipline either during the Millennium or at the Great White Throne judgment, pointing again to the **possibility of post-mortem purification** and **Non-Elect Salvation.**

This lengthy quote from **St. Irenaeus of Lyons**, when examined carefully, significantly **strengthens the possibility of Non-Elect Salvation during the Millennial Reign**, particularly by connecting Matthew 3:11–12's "Baptism by Fire" to a progressive judgment process rather than a single moment of eternal condemnation. Let us examine its core theological implications, keeping to the literal meaning of the words used and the Chiliasm prophecy model.

St. Irenaeus begins by connecting the **passing away of the fashion of this world** with **gathering fruit into the garner** and **burning chaff with fire**—a direct allusion to **Matthew 3:12** and **Malachi 4:1**. He identifies this sequence of events as part of the **Second Coming of Christ**, which leads into the **Millennial Kingdom**, thus confirming once again that the *floor cleansing* by fire is **not instantaneous** but extended through that 1000-year reign.

He explicitly writes: *"when the time of its disappearance has come, in order that the fruit indeed may be gathered into the garner, but the chaff, left behind, may be consumed by fire… He shall baptize you with the Holy Ghost and with fire, having His fan in His hand to cleanse His floor."* This strongly implies that the process of separation and purification **spans a period of time**, not a moment. And even more significantly, he adds that man's **free will** causes him to be either *wheat* or *chaff*—a concept that aligns perfectly with the possibility that someone, though initially chaff, might be transformed into wheat by repentance and the work of this fire.

This aligns tightly with his other quote: *"as fire does chaff, but it purifies all those who are saved, as a fan does wheat."* Here, **the fire is shown to operate in two different modes**: (1) destructive for the chaff, and (2) purifying for the wheat. This naturally harmonizes with **1 Corinthians 3:15**, *"he himself will be saved, yet so as through fire,"* pointing to a salvific effect of divine fire, not reserved only for the Elect, but potentially applicable to others outside that classification.

Interpolated Insight: If fire in this context is both destructive and purifying, and this purification takes place during the Millennial Reign, then this affirms the possibility that some among the *nations*—even those who were not part of the First Resurrection—could be **saved through this fire**. These would not be part of the Church, the *Elect*, who are already glorified and changed (no longer flesh and blood, 1 Corinthians 15:50), but rather others who are judged afterward and yet find mercy.

This is reinforced by the fact that **Revelation 21:6 and 22:17** speak of *those who thirst* being invited to drink from the **Water of Life freely**—and this **invitation comes from the Bride** (i.e. the Church) to those who are outside her. If the Church is already glorified and reigning, the invitation must be going out **to those still in need of salvation**, likely judged and purified during or after the Millennium. In other words, **post-Millennial salvation** is offered to those who come to desire it—*"Whoever desires, let him take the water of life freely."*

Further supporting this possibility is the quote attributed to **St. Ambrose of Milan**:

> "Blessed is he that hath part in the first resurrection, for such come to grace without the judgment. As for those who do not come to the first, but are reserved unto the second resurrection, these shall be disciplined until their appointed times, between the first and the second resurrection."

This distinction between **first** and **second resurrection** lines up with Revelation 20 and the Chiliasm model. The first group (the Elect) reign with Christ, escaping judgment altogether (John 5:24), while the second group (those not in the first resurrection) are **disciplined**, not destroyed, during the Millennium—another clear pointer to **Non-Elect Salvation possibility** through purification.

Also, when Irenaeus says man can become **either wheat or chaff** due to free will, this opens the door for some who were initially chaff to repent and be converted, especially under divine judgment and visible rule of Christ during the 1000 years. This is consistent with **John 6:40**, where Christ affirms that *"everyone who sees the Son and believes in Him may have everlasting life"*—and this refers to being *raised up at the Last Day*, not necessarily at the First Resurrection. It suggests that **seeing and believing** can occur **during the Millennium**, once Christ has returned, which would logically apply to those outside the Church who come to repentance then.

Finally, St. Irenaeus reaffirms bodily resurrection *"at the last trumpet"* (1 Corinthians 15:52), not just spiritual allegory, and connects it with **John 5:28–29**, where **both righteous and wicked** are raised for **life or judgment**. This dual resurrection at the end of the Millennium corresponds with Revelation 20:11–15. But his comments about **those who opposed Christ** being raised in **identical bodies**—not glorified—point to **a different group than the Bride**, who were glorified a thousand years earlier.

If that group includes *surprised sheep* (Matthew 25:31–40), judged by how they treated *His Brethren*, then they were not Christians (His Brethren are Christians). This again implies **post-Millennial salvation** not based on faith during mortal life, but on acts of mercy and perhaps a *new faith* kindled after seeing Christ during judgment.

This quote from St. Irenaeus of Lyons deeply supports the theological structure for **Non-Elect Salvation possibility**, grounded in literal Chiliasm prophecy. It reveals a post-Second Coming process of judgment and purification that extends throughout the Millennium and culminates in some being saved **after** enduring the fire of judgment. These are not part of the Bride but may become **citizens of the renewed earth** under Christ's eternal rule, drinking freely from the water of life.

St. Clement of Alexandria's extensive reflection on **Matthew 3:11–12**—along with related themes of Christ's Shepherding, Fire of Judgment, and chastisement of sinners—appears to support the **possibility of Non-Elect Salvation**, though he never explicitly teaches it as dogma. Nevertheless, his language and imagery offer a consistent framework with the earlier Chiliasm Church Fathers like St. Justin and St. Irenaeus, particularly when it comes to **post-mortem purification** in the **spirit world** and a clear **distinction between Elect and Others** among the saved.

Let us carefully examine and draw the implications of each part of his quote, beginning with his understanding of **Matthew 3:12's fan and fire imagery**:

> "For the fan is in the Lord's hand, by which the chaff due to the fire is separated from the wheat... Feed us, the children, as sheep... on Your holy mountain the Church, which... touches heaven."

This language clearly draws a **twofold picture**. On the one hand, the **Elect** are presented as **children/sheep** already being fed in **heaven**, described metaphorically as the **Church towering above the clouds**—a likely image of the glorified Church, His Bride. On the other hand, the **separation of wheat from chaff** via **fire** implies a **post-mortem judgment** that continues outside that heavenly fold, affecting others—perhaps still redeemable.

What follows builds the distinction further:

> "Promising to give His life a ransom for many... when He might have been Lord, He wished to be a brother man..."

Clement stresses Christ's universal gift: not for **few** (which would describe the **Elect**, cf. Matthew 7:14) but for **many**, mirroring Matthew 20:28. The tone here shifts toward **general human salvation**, especially when he says:

> "So that we may not continue intractable and sinners to the end, and thus fall into condemnation, but may be separated from the chaff, and stored up in the paternal garner."

Here, he leaves open the possibility that some **who are now intractable sinners** may not **remain** so but instead be **separated from the chaff** at the time of judgment. This separation is depicted as happening *at the point of condemnation*, not beforehand—thus possibly after death. This suggests a **refining fire**—not necessarily eternal destruction—for some who were not faithful in this life.

Clement's deeper insight unfolds where he compares men to **iron shaped on the anvil**, healed by **"rebuke and censure"**, even **threatening and chastisement**. He writes:

> "Some are ill to cure, and, like iron, are wrought into shape with fire, and hammer, and anvil... while others... grow by praise."

This comparison explicitly divides people into two groups: (1) **those saved by reproof and fire** and (2) **those saved by faith and virtue**. This division corresponds with (1) the **possible non-elect saved through judgment**, and (2) the **elect saved by faith without further need for purification**. The implication is clear: **salvation is not achieved by the same path for all.**

This interpretation is reinforced in his most mysterious passage:

> "And other sheep there are also... deemed worthy of another fold and mansion, in proportion to their faith... he must put off the passions... The greatest torments, indeed, are assigned to the believer... the punishments cease... in the expiation and purification of each one."

Here, Clement explicitly outlines an **afterlife purification**. Several key observations must be made:

1. The **"other fold"** is not the Church. It is described as **"another mansion"**, lower and inferior.

2. Those in this fold still receive **God's mercy** but undergo **torment**—not endless but **purifying and expiatory**.

3. This happens after they "quit the flesh," meaning **post-mortem**, in the **Spirit World**.

4. Their final grief is **permanent** because they are **not glorified** like the Elect and **miss out** on that union, though they are not destroyed.

These are not "unsaved" in the sense of eternal condemnation, yet they are clearly **excluded from the glorified Church**. That separation—*from the glorified to the lesser fold*—fits the **Non-Elect Salvation possibility**, where some are **redeemed by fire** but do not become part of **the Bride**.

Finally, Clement brings all this together under the theme of **Christ's Ransom for many**—again, **not just the few**. He appears to suggest that the **Elect are the few**, the **Bride**, while the **many** include the **other sheep**, disciplined and purified, and placed in a separate, though still blessed, estate.

This affirms the Chiliasm model's framework:

- The **Bride** participates in the **First Resurrection** and enters the heavenly kingdom.

- The **others**, outside the Church's glorified fold, undergo **post-mortem purification** and may receive **salvation by fire**—as the **"sheep of another fold."**

- These may be the ones hinted at in **Revelation 22:17**, where the **Bride** calls out to those who still thirst to take the water of life freely.

- Clement's own language, comparing chastisement and purification with **healing and reshaping**, reveals God's **disciplinary mercy**, not everlasting torment.

This quote may not conclusively prove Non-Elect Salvation, but it certainly provides strong theological support for its **possibility** in light of post-apostolic faith, especially when combined with the teachings of St. Justin, St. Irenaeus, and others.

This conclusion harmonizes the many threads drawn from early Christian writings, Biblical prophecies, and the consistent testimony of the **Chiliasm Church Fathers**, resulting in a strong and reasoned possibility for **Non-Elect Salvation via Baptism by Fire**. Let us restate and solidify the key theological and prophetic framework undergirding this conclusion.

The doctrine of the **"Baptism by Fire"**—when read plainly in **Matthew 3:11–12**—was taken literally by the earliest fathers to describe a **judgmental and purifying fire** initiated not at Pentecost, but at the **Second Coming of Christ**. This purifying fire is not merely symbolic; it **separates**, tests, **refines**, and even **saves**—not immediately in every case, but **after a duration of purification**, either in Hades or the Spirit World, and during the **Millennial Reign** of Christ, culminating at the **Great White Throne Judgment**.

St. Justin of Rome, St. Irenaeus of Lyons, Tertullian, St. Gregory Nazianzus, St. Ambrose of Milan, and **St. Clement of Alexandria**—whether each saw the details identically or not—all give **credibility** to this broader understanding. Not all specify when or how this "salvation by fire" occurs, but when their testimony is collated, it paints a strong prophetic picture:

Tertullian speaks of the faithful being baptized "in fire unto judgment" if their faith is **pretended or weak**, linking that judgment directly to a **Spirit World prison** from which one is released only after full payment. He suggests that some rise late in the First Resurrection, possibly only after enduring such a purging process—thus missing the Wedding of the Lamb.

St. Irenaeus, while emphasizing two advents of Christ, connects Matthew 3:12's fire with His **Second Coming**, placing the **cleansing of His floor** (i.e. the world) and the burning of chaff within the **Millennial Reign**. His own words support that **some wheat are purified**—not just gathered—and that this purification may span the duration of Christ's reign. His refusal to allegorize, and his insistence on literal resurrection in bodily form, further validates that some are saved **after fire** during this **earthly kingdom**.

St. Gregory Nazianzus affirmed that **baptism by fire** may benefit even those who were **unbaptized by water**, applying it as a **purging postmortem event**, not as final condemnation.

St. Clement of Alexandria, perhaps most explicit in this regard, differentiates between the **Elect**—those already glorified and fed in heavenly Jerusalem—and **others**, the "sheep of another fold" who suffer "great torment" and purification **after quitting the flesh**. He describes their outcome as a **separate, lesser fold**—not destruction—implying **Non-Elect Salvation** distinct from the Elect Bride.

St. Ambrose of Milan, though somewhat later, affirms two resurrections: one of the **blessed without judgment**, and another of those who are **disciplined** and purified **between** the first and second resurrection. He thus offers a clear structural affirmation of the possibility that **some are saved during the 1000 years**, not before.

Even **Isaiah 24:20–23**, a clear **Chiliasm prophecy**, supports this sequence. The earth is shaken, kings are punished, prisoners are shut up in the pit during the Lord's reign on Mount Zion, and then—**after many days**—they are **visited**. The word "visited" (פָּקַד *paqad*) can mean to **inspect**, **punish**, or even **deliver**, allowing room for the interpretation that **some imprisoned are later released**, in line with purgation unto salvation.

Zechariah 13:8–9 offers further detail of this **Millennial Fire**, emphasizing a **refinement** process. Two-thirds perish, but one-third is **brought through the fire**, and ultimately calls on Jehovah's Name—clearly describing the **salvation of some who are purified**, not condemned.

This supports the interpolation that **some of the wheat** is only gathered **after purification**, fitting **1 Corinthians 3:15's** description that "he himself will be saved, yet so as through fire." Such a one does not receive reward but still receives **mercy**.

Lastly, **Revelation 22:17** portrays the **Bride (Elect Church)** as already glorified yet **still calling** to the **thirsty**—those not yet saved—to take of the **Water of Life freely**, consistent with John 6:40, where "everyone who sees the Son and believes in Him" may still be raised **on the Last Day**. If the **Last Day** spans the 1000 years of Christ's Reign as Chiliasm teaches, then **some will believe after seeing**, and be saved, albeit as **Non-Elect**.

Therefore, while **Elect Salvation** pertains to the **First Resurrection** (Revelation 20:4–6), glorification, and the **heavenly inheritance**, the Baptism by Fire may be the **mechanism** through which **some among the non-elect** are eventually **saved** by God's Mercy after judgment. This position does not contradict Scripture but rather **complements** the consistent literal testimony of the earliest Fathers.

SUMMARY

Whenever a **Chiliasm Church Father quote** is absent for a particular Bible verse in this chapter, it is because **no direct quote** could be located for that reference. In every such instance, I have exercised caution to **avoid private interpretation of prophecy**, always seeking to let the historical testimony of early Christian writings take priority.

The **interpolations presented** in this chapter are **original discoveries** resulting from careful **independent research** and direct analysis of available primary sources. If similar views have been published elsewhere using the same language or doctrinal meaning, such agreement would be purely **coincidental**, as nothing here has been copied or plagiarized.

Portions of the discussion also address **commonly held interpretations** among certain Protestant groups, such as **post-tribulation rapture** positions among some **Reformed theologians**. However, this essay emphasizes previously unexplored or rarely argued positions, such as:

1. Two kinds of final resurrection bodies are implied—**heavenly (Elect)** and **earthly (Non-Elect)**—each suited to their respective inheritance, one in the New Heavens and the other in the New Earth.

2. Two distinct groups partake of the Water of Life, separated by the **1000-year Millennial Reign of Christ**. The Elect receive it at the **start** of the Millennium (Revelation 21:6), and a second group—the "thirsty"— receive it at the **end** (Revelation 22:17), possibly those who were in darkness and prison (Isaiah 49:9–10) and are shown mercy after Spirit World Judgment.

3. John 5's resurrection language is best understood with **parabolic timing references**: "the hour now is" refers to the **beginning** of the Millennium, and "the hour is coming" to its **end**. The "hour" is a segment within the "Last Day," which is the entire **1000-year reign**.

4. Matthew's "last penny" judgment parables may allow for **Non-Elect Salvation**, as many Church Fathers acknowledged these as post-mortem, corrective punishments. If even **wicked servants** and **unbelievers** (Luke 12:46–48) can be assigned different punishments, then some might be **saved by fire**, if God so wills.

5. 1 Thessalonians 4:17 and 1 Corinthians 15:52 describe two **distinct events**, separated by **1000 years**: the former at Christ's **Second Coming** (Rapture and First Resurrection), and the latter at the **end of the Millennium**, linked to the **Second Resurrection**.

6. Humanity is divided into three categories: righteous, sinners, and the **wicked**—not merely a binary of saved vs. damned. This triadic classification allows for a middle group that might be saved but **not glorified**, assigned to the **New Earth** rather than the **New Heavens**.

7. Matthew 19's twofold reply to the rich man may distinguish between **Non-Elect Salvation** (commandments concerning man) and **Elect Salvation** (higher calling to discipleship, self-denial, and the Charity Doctrine). Christ's answer implies **gradations of salvation**, not salvation by works, but by **capacity to follow**, whether by faith or by **believing after seeing**.

8. The Book of 1Enoch, viewed through a Chiliasm lens, may place its **change prophecy** at the **end** of the 1000 years (Judgment Day), not its beginning. The second resurrection is a **bodily resurrection for judgment**, where **some are saved without honor**, distinct from the **glorified Elect**.

9. The Shepherd of Hermas, long regarded as Scripture by early Christians, may refer to a **salvation outside the Tower**, suggesting a **Non-Elect Salvation** in the New Earth. This includes **unbaptized hearers** who lapsed into wickedness yet may still receive mercy. **Tertullian's opposition** to Pope Callixtus I over this may reflect discomfort with such implications but affirms that this passage was already well known.

10. 1 Corinthians 3:15's "saved by fire" is newly interpreted here to refer to **someone with no reward at all**, thus **not fitting even the lowest thirtyfold harvest** (Matthew 13:8). This differs from those with reward (1 Corinthians 3:14) and potentially represents **Non-Elect Salvation**. It is mapped to Matthew 3:11–12's **Baptism by Fire**, as elaborated through the Church Fathers.

11. Revelation 21 and **Revelation 22** may contain **three categories**: **Elect Salvation**, **Non-Elect Salvation**, and the **Damned**, contrary to common readings that see only two. In the "Final Scene" (Revelation 22:17), the **Bride calls out** to the **thirsty**, distinct from the unbelieving cast into the Lake of Fire (Revelation 21:8), perhaps suggesting **some who desire salvation** are still offered the Water of Life.

12. John 10:16's "sheep not of this fold" may represent those saved at the **Second Resurrection**, i.e., **Sheepfold2**, as distinct from **Sheepfold1**, the Elect who partake in the First Resurrection. This view counters even other Chiliasm positions which assert that **all of the Second Resurrection** are damned. This new model explains the surprise of these "sheep" on Judgment Day (Matthew 25:31–40), who did not realize they were serving Christ through their charity toward His brethren.

As a final reflection, **Psalm 19:12** captures the spirit of this research effort: **"Who can understand his errors? Cleanse me from secret faults."**

I have tried to lay out the doctrine plainly and truthfully, carefully marking out what is Scripture, what is patristic testimony, and what is personal **interpolation**. I submit it all with humility, knowing that **if these interpretations are false**, they must fall away, and if **true**, they must conform to the judgment of Scripture and the righteousness of God.

APPENDIX An Important Note on Methodology

If you have noticed, in these **Chiliasm writings**, I have not said that these interpretations were given by **God's Grace**, because I am not certain how accurate they are. If any of my **interpolations** turn out to be false on **Judgment Day**, then how could such errors bring glory to God? For this reason, I have presented these interpretations **cautiously** as **personal prophetic possibilities**, not as dogma.

As stated in earlier writings, **Jeremiah 23:36–40** allows the concept of making a **prophetic attempt**, as long as it is not falsely attributed to God. If these things turn out correct on that Day, then and only then will I ascribe all **glory to God** for revealing them in His mercy. Until then, I must not **prematurely claim prophetic certainty**, but rather present each point with supporting **Chiliasm Church Father quotes** to demonstrate that any ambiguity has been handled with integrity through preserved Christian history. I rest my case here.

Among the most intriguing sources are the **Non-Elect Salvation quotes** from the *Shepherd of Hermas*, a work regarded as **Scripture-level** by **St. Irenaeus of Lyons** and **Tertullian**—both solid witnesses within the Chiliasm tradition. For instance, in the **Non-Elect Salvation** section (pp. 27–28), even **Tertullian** himself struggled with the implications of these passages. Yet this very struggle proves that those controversial sections have been **preserved faithfully**, as Tertullian doesn't deny their authenticity, only their interpretation.

Notice Tertullian's response in his debate with **Pope Callixtus I**, where he challenges the *Shepherd of Hermas* due to its apparent support of some kind of salvation for **adulterers** (implied), and yet—despite his disagreement—he concludes as follows:

> "But I would yield my ground to you, if the scripture of the Shepherd, which is the only one which favours adulterers, had deserved to find a place in the Divine canon; if it had not been habitually judged by every council of Churches (even of your own) among apocryphal and false (writings); … I, however, imbibe the Scriptures of that Shepherd who cannot be broken."

This is exemplary **academic honesty**. He acknowledges its standing as Scripture despite his unease. That is the **methodology** I have followed: **sober, evidence-based commentary**, without overstating what is not clear, and always grounded in **verifiable documentation**. Regardless of one's agreement or disagreement with the *Shepherd of Hermas*, the **historical rigor** remains intact.

The Bible itself shows that even **Spirit-filled believers** may differ in doctrine and sharp disagreements may arise. **Acts 15:1–5** records a direct confrontation between **Christian brothers** over salvation and Mosaic Law. One side was wrong, and the issue had to be brought before the apostles. This proves that **God permits doctrinal diversity temporarily**, and **He will reward the more accurate view** later.

So, what benefit is academic prestige if our interpretations turn out wrong—especially in eternal matters such as **Non-Elect Salvation**? I have taken care to ground each proposal in actual quotes from **Chiliasm Church Fathers**, avoiding speculation where no primary evidence is found. That is why I call these interpolations **possibilities**, not doctrines, so that no one is misled.

Readers are encouraged to examine arguments **both for and against** these claims, and to remain **neutral** if unsure. Either way, they are accountable for their response to the evidence. This book has no hidden sources. Whether drawn from **internet translations** or **hardcopy volumes**, these quotes are already **well-known and publicly available**, usually through standard English translations accepted as **faithful to the original languages**. Unless one can demonstrate how reading the Greek or Latin alters the meaning of these translated quotes, the English stands sufficient for interpretation.

On that note, many traditional assertions—such as the claim that **St. Irenaeus of Lyons** or other early **Chiliasm Fathers** prayed to **Virgin Mary**—have **no supporting quotes in their own writings**. Assertions like these are often accepted **without primary documentation**, based on editorial assumptions or traditional readings. In contrast, **every claim made in this writing has a quotation or evidence trail**, and when there is none, the position is clearly marked as **interpolation or unknown**.

High-level journals often claim authority through access to **original manuscripts**, but if those manuscripts provide **no definitive answers**, the resulting conclusions remain **equally speculative**. True **scholarly rigor** does not depend on prestige or institutional name, but on **evidence-based**

interpretation. All claims must be traceable to **quoted material** or they are just traditions of men.

To illustrate, a Calvinistic journal once replied to my submission with:

> "Thanks for your submission. I'll take a look at this submission and give you initial feedback by the end of October."

To which I responded:

> "I welcome your feedback. I may give mine too in response to yours should you rebut it so both sides can be well represented."

This is the kind of **fair and open exchange** needed in true academic work.

I do not regard theological supremacy as belonging to any university—not even Harvard—because **eternally significant discoveries** cannot be judged by secular standards. **Daniel 12:3** declares that those who turn many to righteousness will shine like stars forever. That is the only standard that counts. So let us leave behind **racial games, denominational games, gender games**, and **nepotism**, for the **true Judge** does not regard such things.

If **Non-Elect Salvation** turns out to be **false** on that Day, I will humbly accept correction. My sincere prayer is that all who read this will **believe in Christ** whether this doctrine is true or not. Our faith must never rest on the success of a **speculative possibility**, lest it become an idol. However, I am grateful to have brought these **detailed arguments to light**, so that if wrong, it may be evident that it was a **carefully reasoned error**, not reckless conjecture.

A true Christian will cling to Christ **regardless of whether Non-Elect Salvation is true or not.** Only the **reward level** for accuracy may be affected. My labor in this writing is offered as a **research service**, and while I may sell it as a book commercially, I consider the **interpolation parts** to be **freely given** in principle, since I cannot verify them as infallible truth.

If others may profit from fiction and fantasy, what objection is there in publishing **historical and theological research** on **prophecy**? This writing is filled with **quotes from early Christians and Jewish writings**. Even if the interpretations are wrong, the quotations themselves stand true, and God judges justly. Let it be seen that I was **honest with the ambiguity**, faithful to the text, and eager to see the Day of the Lord.

Maranatha! Even so, come Lord Jesus. Amen.

Thank you for reading this!

Abbreviations Used:
CPM = Chiliasm Prophecy Model
NESP = Non-Elect Salvation Possibility

Bibliography

Ballard, Jordan P. *Defending the Doctrine of Hell. Eleutheria: John W. Rawlings School of Divinity Academic Journal* 8, no. 2 (2025).

Bible. Unless noted, all Scripture is taken from the *New King James Version (NKJV)*. Nashville: Thomas Nelson, 1996, c1982. Other translations used are from biblehub.com.

Borchert, G. L. "Matthew 5:48 – Perfection and the Sermon." *Review & Expositor* 89, no. 2 (1992): 265–269.

Calvin, John. *Institutes of the Christian Religion*. Edited by John T. McNeill. Louisville: Westminster John Knox Press, 1960.

Carter, John W. (Jack). "The Cost of Discipleship." *The American Journal of Biblical Theology* 26, no. 12 (March 3, 2025).

Chien, Dinh Van. "Humanistic Thought in Jesus' Sermon on the Eight Beatens." *Pakistan Journal of Life and Social Sciences* 22, no. 2 (2024): 15165–15170.

Chrysostom, John. *Homily 46 on Matthew*. Translated by George Prevost and revised by M. B. Riddle. In *Nicene and Post-Nicene Fathers*, First Series, Vol. 10. Edited by Philip Schaff. Buffalo, NY: Christian Literature Publishing Co., 1888.

Du Toit, Philip La Grange. "The Radical New Perspective on Paul, Messianic Judaism and Their Connection to Christian Zionism." *HTS Theological Studies* 73, no. 3 (2017): 1–8.

Earnhardt, Matthew P. "Exegetical Study of Matthew 19:16–26." *The American Journal of Biblical Theology* (March 10, 2023).

Feldmeier, R. "As Your Heavenly Father Is Perfect: The God of the Bible and Commandments in the Gospel." *Interpretation* 70, no. 4 (2016): 431–444.

Herberg, Will. "Judaism and Christianity: Their Unity and Difference. The Double Covenant in the Divine Economy of Salvation." *Journal of Bible and Religion* 21, no. 2 (1953): 67–78.

Inserra, Dean. *The Unsaved Christian: Reaching Cultural Christianity with the Gospel*. Chicago: Moody Publishers, 2019.

Irenaeus of Lyons. *Against Heresies*. Translated by Alexander Roberts and William Rambaut. In *Ante-Nicene Fathers*, Vol. 1. Edited by Alexander Roberts, James Donaldson, and A. Cleveland Coxe. Buffalo, NY: Christian Literature Publishing Co., 1885.

Justin of Rome (Justin Martyr). *Dialogue with Trypho*. Translated by Marcus Dods and George Reith. In *Ante-Nicene Fathers*, Vol. 1. Edited by Alexander Roberts, James Donaldson, and A. Cleveland Coxe. Buffalo, NY: Christian Literature Publishing Co., 1885.

————. *The First Apology*. Translated by Marcus Dods and George Reith. In *Ante-Nicene Fathers*, Vol. 1. Edited by Alexander Roberts, James Donaldson, and A. Cleveland Coxe. Buffalo, NY: Christian Literature Publishing Co., 1885.

Kolb, Robert, and Timothy J. Wengert, eds. *The Book of Concord: The Confessions of the Evangelical Lutheran Church*. Minneapolis: Fortress Press, 2000.

Koplitz, Michael. "Hebraic Analysis for Matthew 19:27–30" (2020).

Korver, Bill Fredric. "Biblical Use of Rewards as a Motivation for Christian Service." PhD diss., Liberty University, 2011.

Lactantius. *Divine Institutes*. Translated by William Fletcher. In *Ante-Nicene Fathers*, Vol. 7. Edited by Alexander Roberts, James Donaldson, and A. Cleveland Coxe. Buffalo, NY: Christian Literature Publishing Co., 1886.

MacArthur, John. *Hard to Believe: The High Cost and Infinite Value of Following Jesus*. Nashville, TN: Nelson, 2003.

O'Collins, G. "Difficult Texts: Being Made Perfect According to Matthew 5 and 19." *Theology* 124, no. 6 (2021): 404–409.

Ramachandran, Jonathan. "Non-Elect Salvation Possibility (NESP)." *The American Journal of Biblical Theology* 26, no. 6 (February 9, 2025).

Richardson, James. "Quotes from Early Church Fathers: The Sabbath, Lord's Day, and Worship – Apostles Creed." *Apostles Creed*, August 10, 2016.

Shepherd, Thomas R. "The Parable of the Rich Man and Lazarus: A Narrative-Exegetical Study of Its Relationship to the Afterlife, Wealth, and Poverty – Part 1: The Afterlife." *Journal of the Adventist Theological Society* 32, nos. 1–2 (2021): 171–189.

Stevenson, L. "On the Very Idea of Perfection." *International Journal of Philosophy and Theology* 85, nos. 3–4 (2024): 111–123.

Tanasyah, Yusak. "The Development of Hell from Jewish to Christian Theology: A Biblical Guide to Hell and Its Existence." *QUAERENS: Journal of Theology and Christianity Studies* 4, no. 1 (2022): 27–41.

Tertullian. *A Treatise on the Soul.* Translated by Peter Holmes. In *Ante-Nicene Fathers*, Vol. 3. Edited by Alexander Roberts, James Donaldson, and A. Cleveland Coxe. Buffalo, NY: Christian Literature Publishing Co., 1885.

———. *An Answer to the Jews.* Translated by S. Thelwall. In *Ante-Nicene Fathers*, Vol. 3. Edited by Alexander Roberts, James Donaldson, and A. Cleveland Coxe. Buffalo, NY: Christian Literature Publishing Co., 1885.

———. *On Fasting.* Translated by S. Thelwall. In *Ante-Nicene Fathers*, Vol. 4. Edited by Alexander Roberts, James Donaldson, and A. Cleveland Coxe. Buffalo, NY: Christian Literature Publishing Co., 1885.

Vacendak, Robert. "Is Assurance of Salvation of the Essence of Saving Faith in the Gospel of John?" PhD diss., Rawlings School of Divinity, Liberty University, 2023.

Vaught, Carl G. *The Sermon on the Mount: A Theological Interpretation.* Albany, NY: SUNY Press, 1986.

Vries, Simon John De. *From Old Revelation to New: A Tradition-Historical and Redaction-Critical Study of Temporal Transitions in Prophetic Prediction.* Grand Rapids: Wm. B. Eerdmans Publishing, 1995.

Wood, A. Skevington. "The Eschatology of Irenaeus." *The Evangelical Quarterly* 41, no. 1 (January–March 1969).